This is the most important book on feminist criminology since Carol Smart's pioneering text, *Women, Crime and Criminology*, first published in 1976. *Feminist Criminology* is a timely review of the diverse contributions of feminist perspectives to the once gender blind discipline of criminology. This book is a comprehensive yet concise and sophisticated overview of the contribution of feminist perspectives to criminology since the early 1970s. It addresses what lessons have been learnt and what new directions lie ahead in a world where the relevance of feminism is constantly challenged. I commend this book to all students of criminology, serious scholars of crime and justice, as well as practitioners, as gender is still one of the strongest predictors of crime and violence in society today. Read this book to find out why.

—*Professor Kerry Carrington, School of Justice, Queensland University of Technology*

Claire Renzetti has written a remarkable book on feminist criminology that needed to be written, showing how far we've come, but also, where we still need to go. *Feminist Criminology* is interdisciplinary, as it should be, given that criminology and feminism are interdisciplinary. I can't imagine anyone better suited to capture the historical, legal, sociological, and psychological aspects as Renzetti, and she has done so in a manner not only easy to consume, but hard to stop reading.

—*Professor Joanne Belknap, Institute of Behavioral Sciences, University of Colorado*

Claire M. Renzetti has a flair for illuminating a variety of feminist theoretical positions and approaches used to look at criminology. This welcome book explores the diversity of feminist criminological theories, emerging concepts, and their transformative potential for research, practice, and knowledge production. Scholars, teachers, and students will gain valuable insight into how to include gender, race, and class into their analyses as well as how to use feminist criminology to create meaningful public policy.

—Professor Susan L. Miller, Sociology and Criminal Justice, University of Delaware

FEMINIST CRIMINOLOGY

Feminist criminology grew out of the Women's Movement of the 1970s, in response to the male dominance of mainstream criminology – which meant that not only were women largely excluded from carrying out criminological research, they were also barely considered as subjects of that research.

In this volume, Claire M. Renzetti traces the development of feminist criminology from the 1970s to the present, examining the diversity of feminisms which have developed:

- liberal feminist criminology
- Marxist, radical, and socialist feminist criminologies
- structured action theory
- left realism
- postmodern feminism
- black/multiracial feminist criminology.

She shows how these perspectives have made a great impact on the discipline, the academy, and the criminal justice system, but also highlights the limitations of this influence. How far has feminist criminology *transformed* research and knowledge production, education, and practice? And how can feminist criminologists continue to shape the future of the discipline?

Claire M. Renzetti is the Judi Conway Patton Endowed Chair in the Center for Research on Violence Against Women, and Professor of Sociology, at the University of Kentucky. She is editor of the journal *Violence Against Women*; co-editor of the 'Interpersonal Violence' book series for Oxford University Press; and editor of the 'Gender, Crime and Law' book series for Northeastern University Press. Her recent research focuses on religiosity and intimate partner violence, and the provision of services for domestic sex trafficking victims.

KEY IDEAS IN CRIMINOLOGY

SERIES EDITOR: TIM NEWBURN is Professor of Criminology and Social Policy, Director of the Mannheim Centre for Criminology, London School of Economics and President of the British Society of Criminology. He has written and researched widely on issues of crime and justice.

Key Ideas in Criminology explores the major concepts, issues, debates, and controversies in criminology. The series aims to provide authoritative essays on central topics within the broader area of criminology. Each book adopts a strong individual 'line', constituting original essays rather than literature surveys, and offers lively and agenda setting treatments of its subject matter.

These books will appeal to students, teachers and researchers in criminology, sociology, social policy, cultural studies, law, and political science.

Titles in the series:

Penal Populism
John Pratt

Rehabilitation
Tony Ward and Shadd Maruna

Security
Lucia Zedner

Surveillance
Benjamin Goold

Genocidal Crimes
Alex Alvarez

Public Criminology?
Ian Loader and Richard Sparks

Contemporary Critical Criminology
Walter S. DeKeseredy

Feminist Criminology
Claire M. Renzetti

Sentencing
Ralph Henham

Crime News
Chris Greer

Policing
Michael Kempa and Clifford Shearing

FEMINIST CRIMINOLOGY

Claire M. Renzetti

Routledge
Taylor & Francis Group
LONDON AND NEW YORK

First published 2013
by Routledge
2 Park Square, Milton Park, Abingdon, Oxon OX14 4RN

Simultaneously published in the USA and Canada
by Routledge
711 Third Avenue, New York, NY 10017

Routledge is an imprint of the Taylor & Francis Group, an informa business

British Library Cataloguing in Publication Data
A catalogue record for this book is available from the British Library

Library of Congress Cataloging in Publication Data
Renzetti, Claire M.
Feminist criminology / Claire M. Renzetti.
pages cm. — (Key ideas in criminology)
Includes bibliographical references and index.
1. Criminology. 2. Feminism. 3. Women—Crimes against.
I. Title.
HV6030.R45 2013
364.082—dc23 2012046500

ISBN: 978-0-415-38143-7 (hbk)
ISBN: 978-0-415-38142-0 (pbk)
ISBN: 978-0-203-93031-1 (ebk)

Typeset in Garamond 3
by RefineCatch Limited, Bungay, Suffolk

Printed and bound by CPI Group (UK) Ltd, Croydon, CR0 4YY

To the members of the Division on Women and Crime of the American Society of Criminology: I am thankful for your collegiality over these many years and, even more, I am grateful for your friendship.

Contents

List of tables

Preface

This book began to take shape in 2004. I was asked to participate on a Past President's Panel on the "Present and Future Status of Criminology" at the annual meeting of the American Society of Criminology (ASC). My talk focused on the extent to which feminist criminologists had succeeded in reforming, if not revolutionizing, "mainstream" criminology. While noting important changes to the field, I nonetheless emphasized the limited nature of this progress, hoping to cajole those in attendance – besides my many friends from the ASC Division on Women and Crime who had come to support me – to move beyond merely "tolerating" feminist criminology and criminologists and instead incorporate gender, race, and class analyses into *all* criminological research, making such analyses mainstream rather than marginal. As I left the meeting room, I was stopped by a tall man with a warm smile and lovely German accent, who introduced himself as Gerhard Boomgaarden, an editor for Routledge. Gerhard wanted to know if I would be interested in expanding my talk into a book on feminist criminology for Tim Newburn's *Key Ideas in Criminology* series. Although I was very flattered that he and Tim would consider my work for the series, and this was definitely a topic on which I had long wanted to write a book, I quickly and firmly said no. I was already overcommitted, I told him, with other writing projects, teaching and professional service responsibilities, an elderly and ill mother, a weekly commute by plane to work, and other major changes in my personal life. Still smiling, Gerhard only grew more animated and talked more rapidly – I would swear he was bouncing a little on the balls of his feet – and he offered a good retort to every one of my objections. By the time we parted, I had agreed to send him a prospectus for the book.

Although he would never admit to it publicly because he is too much of a professional, I have often wondered in the intervening years if Gerhard regretted making such a fine sales pitch that day. After all, it has taken me quite a lot of time to finally get this slim volume into print. Throughout this process, though, Gerhard has been patient and supportive and encouraging. He never once told me any of my excuses for missing yet another deadline (that he had graciously let me set myself) were lousy or even flimsy. And he never stopped smiling – at least not in front of me. I consider myself very fortunate to have had such an editor for this project, and even more fortunate that he has become a friend. To him, I owe the largest dose of gratitude. To Tim Newburn, too, I extend my thanks for never giving up on me. And to Emily Briggs, editorial assistant, I express my gratitude for her advice and support, and especially for her cheerful email messages, throughout the publication process.

Of course, I have many colleagues and friends to thank for their support of this endeavor (and others). I wish to thank Frank Scarpitti for inviting me to participate on the Past President's Panel in 2004 and for everything he's taught me, starting with my first criminology course. (The year I took that course need not be specified.) I also thank Joann Belknap, Denise Boots, Susan Caringella, Kim Cook, Meda Chesney-Lind, Walter DeKeseredy, Jeff Edleson, Kathleen Ferraro, Angela Gover, Susan Miller, and Marty Schwartz for countless email exchanges, conversations, collaborations, and an unwavering willingness to help me out whenever I ask. I don't want to even try to tally the number of manuscripts that you all have reviewed for me. A special word of thanks is in order for Raquel Bergen. Raquel was one of my undergraduate students at St. Joseph's University in the 1980s, later became my colleague in the sociology department there, and eventually became my department chair. I've had the pleasure to work with her on several writing projects, and our collaboration continues. Most important, she is my friend extraordinaire. I thank her for her sharp intellect and her even sharper sense of humor, both of which have seen me through a number of vexing problems.

Finally, I thank my colleagues in the Sociology Department, and Carol Jordan, Ann Coker, Diane Follingstad, and Charley Carlson, my colleagues in the Center for Research on Violence Against Women, at the University of Kentucky, for welcoming me warmly to my new academic home. I am delighted to be part of the team.

1

FEMINIST CRIMINOLOGY

A BRIEF OVERVIEW

"What does it mean to be a feminist criminologist?" The student's question made me pause. It wasn't that I didn't have an answer; I did. In fact, I had a succinct, pre-packaged answer at the ready, because I was often asked, "What is feminist criminology?" But this was the first time the question was phrased this way, and although I quickly delivered my pat response in class that day, I realized that there are many answers to the question of what it *means to be a feminist* criminologist – answers that are as diverse as feminist criminologists themselves and that have changed considerably over the past 35 years. This book, then, is my long answer to the student's question. In this volume, I will trace the development of feminist criminology from the 1970s to the present, considering along the way the diversity of feminisms in criminology as well as the impact these perspectives have had in various arenas: the discipline, the academy, and the criminal justice system. I will conclude with a discussion of what I consider to be major emerging trends in feminist criminology and offer an assessment of feminist criminologists' potential for shaping the future of our discipline.

In the pages that follow, we examine a great deal of evidence indicating that in a relatively short period of time, feminist criminologists have made a substantial impact on criminological theory and research methods; on curriculum, pedagogy, and the campus climate for faculty and students; and on the practice of law and criminal justice. At the same time, we will also see the limitations of this influence and question the extent to which feminist criminology has *transformed* research and knowledge production, education, and practice. There is no doubt that things have changed – and for the better – but we also have no hesitation in quoting the well-worn adage that the more things have changed, the more they have stayed the same. Consequently, we cannot neglect the question of where do we go – where do we want to go – from here?

Before undertaking this discussion, however, we must first lay the foundation by defining two key concepts: *feminist* and *criminology*. Despite theoretical differences across the field, most criminologists would agree that a basic definition of *criminology* is the study of crime, criminal behavior, and social control. To be sure, there would be far less consensus regarding the definitions of crime and criminal behavior and, therefore, of what needs to be controlled and how – a point that is addressed throughout this book (see, for example, Bosworth and Hoyle, 2011). What about the adjective (and noun) *feminist*? A recent research experience highlighted for me the confusion – as well as the social and political baggage – that plagues this term. In conducting interviews with social activists working to address the problem of human trafficking, I posed the question, "Do you consider yourself a feminist?" The typical response from the interviewees was something along the lines of, "No, I wouldn't say I'm a feminist because I think all people should be treated equally and with respect." Such replies betray a basic misunderstanding of feminism. The remainder of this chapter, then, examines the emergence of contemporary feminism and presents several principles that form the core of feminist criminology. We are then better equipped to explore diverse feminist criminological perspectives and their influence in subsequent chapters.

FEMINISM IN HISTORICAL PERSPECTIVE

The development of feminism as a theoretical framework as well as a social movement is typically discussed in terms of historical periods or "waves." Most historians identify the first wave of feminism as the period 1830–1920, but others have identified ideas and activities that they consider feminist going back to early Christianity, the Middle Ages, the Renaissance, and the Reformation (LeGates, 2001; Lerner, 1993). This feminism primarily took the form of individual women rebelling against sexist gender norms, but because these women were largely unaware that others were resisting too, a feminist consciousness – that is, an awareness by women that they were treated unequally as a group and that their subordination was socially created and maintained by a system that could be changed through collective action – did not develop. Consequently, while examples of individual feminist *resistance* can be found throughout history, feminism as a *paradigm* for explaining social relations and as a *social movement* did not emerge until around the turn of the nineteenth century.

In the United States, Great Britain, and Europe, early feminist activism focused largely on winning various legal rights for women given that they did not enjoy full citizenship the way men did. Initially, the goals included better legal protection of women and children from abuse, marriage and divorce reforms, equal access to education and improved employment opportunities, and revisions to property laws.[1] As the movement grew, however, and encountered strong resistance from law makers, the focus narrowed, especially in the United States, to the right to vote, the argument being that if women had the power to elect law makers, the law makers would have to become more responsive to women's demands (Cott, 1987; Lovenduski, 1986; Offen, 1988; Rupp and Taylor, 1999).

The women involved in the first wave of feminism were primarily white and middle or upper class. Ironically, it was not uncommon for them to exploit sexist and racist stereotypes to try to win support for their cause. In the United States, for example, feminists had strong ties to the anti-slavery or abolitionist movement, but when black men were enfranchised by the Fifteenth Amendment to the Constitution and women were excluded, some feminists sought support for women's suffrage by arguing it was needed to counteract black voting power. Others capitalized on growing anti-immigrant sentiment among native-born whites with similar arguments. And the claim that women should vote because they would "purify politics" with their innate nurturance and higher standards of morality was also commonly marshaled in favor of women's suffrage (Cott, 1987; "Suffragette's Racial Remark," 1996).

This is not to say that there were no more radical feminists during the first wave of the movement. Charlotte Perkins Gilman, for example, organized working-class women and men and new citizens into voting organizations (Cott, 1986), and black women's organizations also offered civics classes to prepare women for enfranchisement (Hine and Thompson, 1997). Black women, in particular, were concerned not only with the right to vote for themselves, but also with preventing the violent subversion of black men's voting rights and with addressing the racism being mustered on behalf of white women's enfranchisement (Cott, 1986, 1987). Without doubt, "mainstream feminism" during this period was not a movement for every woman, but rather explicitly for white, middle-class and wealthier women.

The extent to which first-wave feminists were successful in achieving their goals depended to a large degree on conditions in specific countries. In many European countries, for instance, divorce laws were liberalized during the nineteenth and early twentieth centuries, but in countries strongly identified with the Roman Catholic church, divorce continued to be prohibited until relatively recently. Success in enfranchising women also varied significantly, with many countries giving women the right to vote during or shortly after World War I (e.g. Austria, Belgium, Canada, Denmark, Germany, Sweden, the United Kingdom, the United States), whereas others had done so much earlier (e.g. Australia in 1902, Finland in 1906) and a few held out until much later (France in 1944, Italy in 1946, Switzerland in 1971). Ironically, while feminists claimed that giving women the right to vote would solve nearly all social and political problems, women's enfranchisement produced little social change. Fewer women than men exercised their right to vote, and when they voted, they tended to vote similarly to men. Moreover, once enfranchisement was attained, many supporters of feminism lost interest in the movement; they believed gender equality had been won. Historians note that young women were especially hostile to feminism in the conservative postwar years, seeing feminists as lonely, unmarried women who needlessly antagonized men (O'Neill, 1969). So while feminism certainly did not completely disappear (see, for example,

Cott, 1987; Taylor, 1990), the period from 1920 until the early 1960s was not a time of mass feminist mobilization and support.

In the 1960s, several factors contributed to a resurgence of feminist activism, launching what has come to be called feminism's second wave. One was the publication of Betty Friedan's book, *The Feminine Mystique*, in 1963. Friedan gave voice to the dissatisfaction and unhappiness of white, educated, middle-class housewives, isolated in suburbia, who subordinated their own needs and desires to those of their husbands and children, only to be left with a profound lack of personal fulfillment. An exemplar of Mills' (1959) sociological imagination, Friedan's international bestseller presented this "problem that has no name" as a *social* problem, not an individual one. *The Feminine Mystique* became a springboard for developing analyses of sexual politics or, more specifically, the analysis of gender inequality as rooted in both intimate relationships between women and men and in institutional arrangements (Stacey, 1986). It was from these analyses that the much-quoted feminist slogan, "The personal is political," was born.

Even prior to the publication of Friedan's book, however, the U.S. Federal Government had begun to draw attention to the problem of sex discrimination, particularly in employment. In 1961, President John F. Kennedy appointed a Presidential Commission on the Status of Women, whose final report contributed to the passage of the Equal Pay Act of 1963, led to the appointment of two permanent federal committees on women's issues, and became a model for numerous state-level commissions. The state commissions, in turn, contributed to the founding of the National Organization for Women (NOW) in 1966 and other feminist activist groups.

But while *The Feminine Mystique* and NOW strongly resembled first-wave feminist groups in terms of the class and racial identities of their supporters, there was at about the same time a second, more militant branch of feminism forming. This feminism grew out of the political left, from other social movements in the United States, Canada, Great Britain, and Europe that had developed in response to widespread social injustice, including colonialism, racism, and the Vietnam War. Women were active participants in these movements, but quickly (and correctly) realized that they often were not treated as equals by male movement leaders or members. These women activists were struck by the glaring contradiction between the ideology of equality and freedom espoused by radical men and the men's sexist treatment of women (Evans, 1979; Rosen, 2000). Consequently, by the late 1960s, these women had formed their own feminist organizations that were less formally structured and more politically radical than NOW and similar groups, and that focused on developing theoretical analyses of women's subordination and engaging in political activism to end gender oppression (Rosen, ibid.). While this branch of feminism was more diverse than mainstream feminism, it was still dominated by white, educated, and relatively privileged women, and the wielding of these race and class privileges eventually contributed to dissension and fracturing within the movement. Lesbians and women of color, in particular, did not feel these feminists truly understood or accurately represented their interests. As mentioned in Chapter 4, these factions within the movement contributed to the emergence of what some refer to as the "third wave" of feminism.

Like much political and social activism of the 1960s, feminism, particularly the more radical branch of the movement, was centered on university campuses. Not surprisingly, many academics – mostly women, but also some men – began to look not only outward at other social institutions, but also inward at their universities and their disciplines. "How," they asked, "are my campus, my department, and my discipline actively or implicitly reproducing social inequalities, including gender inequality? And what can be done about it?" Criminology was no exception, and this introspection gave rise to multiple perspectives within criminology, all of which answer these questions differently, but all of which are considered feminist. It is these perspectives and their impacts that are the focus of the remainder of this book. As we noted previously, however, there are several core principles that feminist theories share, so we examine them briefly now, saving a discussion of each perspective's riffs on these principles for subsequent chapters.

A FEMINIST FRAMEWORK

At the heart of any feminist theory is the recognition that *gender* is a basic organizational element of social life and social structure.

Feminists maintain that gender is embedded in all social interactions and processes of everyday life as well as all social institutions (Lorber, 2009). The social world, in short, is fundamentally gendered.

This observation, though, begs the question: What is gender? Gender may be defined as the *socially constructed* expectations or norms prescribing female and male attitudes and behavior that are usually organized dichotomously as *femininity* and *masculinity*, respectively, and that are reproduced and transmitted through socialization. Emphasizing the social origins of gender does not mean that feminists ignore the role of biology in influencing gender development. One can hardly deny biological differences between females and males, or overlook the markers of sexual difference in female and male bodies. Feminists instead acknowledge the importance of both biology and culture in the acquisition of gender. A major point, however, is that it is nearly impossible to separate out the precise influences of biology and culture because, for one thing, the socialization process begins as soon as a person is born. Moreover, biology and culture are intertwined in human development over the life course. Biology and culture act on and react to one another. As one scientist explained it, our genes "do not make specific bits and pieces of a body; they code for a range of forms under an array of environmental conditions. . . . [E]ven when a trait has been built and set, environmental intervention may still modify [it]" (Gould, 1981: 156). And, as we discuss in more detail shortly, humans have agency. We may choose, for instance, to modify specific biological traits. Our biology clearly is not our destiny.

Consequently, feminist theorists, especially in the social sciences such as criminology, begin with the assumption that gender is essentially socially created and reproduced, not innately determined and immutable. We are taught the norms of masculinity and femininity, and through this process of social learning these gendered expectations become fundamental components of our personalities. But feminists go a step further, pointing out that this learning as well as the content of gender norms themselves are social products generated within the context of the social structure in which we live. All societies prescribe traits, behaviors, and patterns of social interaction for their members on the basis of sex. And these prescriptions become embedded in the institutions of the society – for example, in family forms, religions, education, the economy, government, and the legal system; they form what feminist theorists refer to as the society's *gender structure*. The gender structure typically functions as a system of social stratification; that is, the traits and behaviors respectively associated with men and women are not valued equally, and men and women do not have equal access to society's resources and rewards. This differential valuing of one gender over the other is called sexism, and sexism manifests as gender discrimination. Sexism, then, occurs both on a macro (structural/institutional) and a micro (interpersonal) level.

In Western societies, and in most societies throughout the world, the gender structure is patriarchal. A *patriarchy* is a gender structure in which men dominate women, and what is considered masculine is more highly valued than what is considered feminine. Given that the academic disciplines exist within this patriarchal structure, it is not surprising that women have been systematically excluded from many fields, including criminology, which are not considered "feminine" or appropriate for women. Women and girls have also been systematically excluded from the studies conducted by members of male-dominated fields, again including criminology, under the assumption that what women do, think, or say is unimportant, uninteresting, or irrelevant (Lorber, 2009). In response to this exclusion, another core principle of feminism is the inclusion of women as professionals and practitioners in all fields, and the inclusion of female experiences and perspectives in theorizing and research.

Beginning in the 1970s in criminology, similar to other disciplines, feminists drew attention to the gender biases in popular criminological theories and highlighted how women and girls historically were overlooked in crime and criminal justice research (Chesney-Lind, 2006; Jurik, 1999). They also documented widespread discrimination against women – in the justice system as both offenders and victims, in the criminal justice and legal professions as practitioners, and in academe generally and in criminology specifically as social scientists and faculty members. As mentioned in Chapter 2, initial attempts to redress this exclusion and discrimination took two forms: first, simply "adding" women to existing theories, to traditional research designs on traditional masculine topics, to various professions (e.g. police, attorneys, corrections officers), to academic departments, and to university committees; and second, showcasing "exceptional" women who had succeeded according to a male standard (Gelsthorpe and Morris, 1988; Goodstein, 1992). It soon became clear, however, that while these efforts were necessary, they were insufficient and ineffective in shifting "the fundamental parameters and masculinity of criminology" (Gelsthorpe and Morris, 1988: 229). What was needed were new theoretical approaches; studies that uncovered and explained the similarities and differences in women's and men's behaviors, attitudes and experiences, arising from their different locations in – and differentially imposed valuing by – the social structure; and a restructuring of social institutions, including the legal system and the academy, to make them gender cognizant and gender equitable.

An examination of the various ways feminist criminologists have undertaken these tasks is the focus of Chapters 3 and 4. For now though more needs to be said about the core feminist principle of including female experiences and perspectives in theorizing and research. It is critically important to state that this insistence on the inclusion of women does not axiomatically require the exclusion of men. Unfortunately, many people, like the interviewees quoted earlier, hold the mistaken impression that feminism is "only" about women or "women's issues." Although feminist theorists and researchers, including feminist criminologists, have unquestionably prioritized the study of women's attitudes, behaviors, and experiences because these have historically been neglected or ignored, feminist perspectives focus on *gender*, including theorizing and studying masculinities as well as femininities. For instance, while criminologists traditionally excluded women from crime studies because women are so much less likely to commit crimes than men, thereby rendering them "uninteresting" or "irrelevant" from a criminological standpoint, feminist criminologists want to know what accounts for gender differences in criminal offending. As mentioned in subsequent chapters, the "gender gap" in criminal offending has frequently been a starting point for feminist criminological research (Britton, 2000).

Through their studies of women's *and* men's lives over nearly four decades, feminist social scientists have demonstrated that the categories "female" and "male" are not homogenous.[2] For example, while men enjoy greater access to resources and rewards in patriarchal societies, not all men benefit equally or in the same ways from gender privilege. Similarly, some groups of women enjoy more gender privilege than other groups of women. Privilege and oppression are not mutually exclusive categories; for example, one may enjoy gender privilege, while simultaneously experiencing racial oppression (Frankenberg, 1993). As feminism has developed and matured, therefore, another core principle that has emerged is the necessity of analyzing how gender inequality intersects with other inequalities, including racism, classism, heterosexism, ageism, and ableism, to form a *matrix of oppression* (Collins, 2000) that impacts women's and men's everyday lives, including their risk of criminal victimization and offending and their treatment as "clients" or employees of the criminal justice system or the academy (Burgess-Proctor, 2006; Risman, 2004). In Chapter 4 we outline how this feminist principle has been applied in criminological theorizing and research.

Feminists' attention to the diversity of women's and men's attitudes, behaviors, and experiences is also evident in the ways they conduct research. Throughout this book we discuss a wide range of feminist criminological studies, but suffice it to say here that, in general, feminist researchers reject the traditional model of science as "establishing mastery over subjects, as demanding the absence of feeling, and as enforcing separateness of the knower from the known, all under the guise of 'objectivity'" (Hess and Ferree, 1987: 13; see also Naples, 2003; Reinharz, 1992; Renzetti, 1997). Feminist research, in contrast, is often characterized by *reciprocity* between the researcher and the research participants.[3] What this means in practice is that rather than establishing relational distance from study participants, the researcher engages in self-disclosure, answering personal questions about themselves that research participants may raise. The researcher may also suggest resources and other helpful information to specific study participants, or offer physical comfort by holding their hand or hugging them if they cry, recognizing that research participants are frequently revealing private, sometimes traumatic aspects of their lives to a stranger – i.e. the researcher – and that they may, in fact, need assistance that the researcher can provide. These situations often arise in research on the kinds of sensitive topics that criminologists study (Bergen, 1993; Campbell *et al.*, 2010; Renzetti and Lee, 1993). Feminist researchers also try to take an *empathic stance* toward the participants in their studies. Instead of imposing their own ideas or response categories on their participants, they may give participants a more active role in guiding the direction of the research and attempt to understand the phenomena they are studying from the participants' points of view (Naples, 2003; Renzetti, 1997).

Feminist researchers' adherence to the principles of reciprocity and empathy in the research process has led to charges of bias by social scientists who work within the traditional positivist paradigm. But this approach to research follows from another core principle of feminist perspectives: The research process is *dualistic*. More specifically, feminist researchers maintain that the research process has both subjective and objective dimensions; there is no completely unbiased or value-free research. Regardless of how objective researchers like to believe themselves to be, they cannot help but be influenced by values, personal preferences, and aspects of the cultural setting and institutional structures in which they live and work. The decision to conduct research and the choice of a research topic are nearly always value-based, reflecting the researcher's appraisal of what is worthy of study. Nevertheless, research is never totally subjective either. Although researchers may be influenced by personal values or judgments, their goal is the collection of facts (i.e. phenomena that can be observed and empirically verified). Feminists challenge themselves and fellow researchers to explicitly acknowledge the assumptions, beliefs, sympathies, and potential biases that may influence their work. They also question not only the possibility, but also the desirability of value-free science, but at the same time, they do not reject scientific standards in their studies (Naples, 2003; Reinharz, 1992).

The feminist emphasis on reciprocity and empathy in research has also led some observers to believe that feminists reject quantitative methodologies in favor of what positivists would tend to call the "soft science" of qualitative methods. Certainly, the principles of reciprocity and an empathic stance are highly compatible with such qualitative methods as ethnography and in-depth interviewing, but many feminist researchers, including feminist criminologists as we mention in subsequent chapters, conduct quantitative studies using sophisticated statistical analyses, or mixed methods that incorporate both quantitative and qualitative techniques (see, for example, Campbell, 2011a, 2011b). Feminist researchers value "multiple ways of knowing" (Jaffe *et al.*, 2011). It is not so much that they distrust quantitative methods per se, but rather that they are wary of how numbers may be used to either justify inequality and oppression, or to devalue or trivialize a problem, particularly a problem that affects women or other oppressed groups. If the numbers are not "big enough," then the problem may not be taken seriously. As Jaffe *et al.* (ibid.: 1164) note, "there is nothing inherently problematic with quantitative methods, but instead the problem lies with how statistics have been used, in some cases, to further exploit or oppress marginalized groups." The decision to use quantitative or qualitative methods or both should depend on "the purpose of the particular study, the questions being asked, and the type of change that is sought" (ibid.).

The latter phrase from Jaffe *et al.* (2011) regarding "the type of change that is sought" brings us to the final core principle of feminism we wish to discuss. Unlike most other perspectives, feminism is not just a theoretical framework. Feminism is a *social movement*, and feminists are scholar activists. They engage in collective action with the goals of eliminating sexism and promoting gender equity in all areas of social life, although the particular methods they use and outcomes they seek vary depending on the specific feminist perspective to which they subscribe. Their activism is tied with their research; they are engaged in what sociologist Joann Miller (2011) calls *purpose-driven research*: that is, research that raises awareness, in this case, of gendered inequalities, and that produces usable knowledge that contributes to the social reconstruction of gender and gender relations that are more equitable. Feminist social scientists, including feminist criminologists, strive to acquire scientific knowledge through the research process that empowers individuals and groups to act to change behaviors and conditions that are harmful or oppressive. Recall the feminist principle that gender, gender relations, and the gender structure are social creations; as such, they can be changed. "[S]ocial structure shapes individuals, but simultaneously, individuals shape the social structure. . . . We must pay attention both to how structure shapes individual choice and social interaction and how human agency creates, sustains, and modifies current structure" (Risman, 2004: 433). In the pages that follow, we examine the various changes to which feminist criminologists have contributed through their scholarship activism – e.g. public recognition of women's violent victimization at the hands of men, the development of victim services as well as gender-conscious offender programs, changes in curriculum, changes in employment in universities and the criminal legal system – and we reflect on the impact of these changes.

FEMINIST CRIMINOLOGIES

Returning to the question that opened this chapter – What does it mean to be a feminist criminologist? – the short answer is that feminist criminology is a paradigm that studies and explains criminal offending and victimization, as well as institutional responses to these problems, as fundamentally gendered, and that emphasizes the importance of using the scientific knowledge we acquire from our study of these issues to influence the creation and implementation of public policy that will alleviate oppression and contribute to more equitable social relations and social structures. But as we also noted at the outset, there is no single, unitary feminist perspective in criminology; there is instead a diversity of feminist perspectives, each with variations on the core principles we have discussed here.

In Chapters 2–4, we examine these various feminist criminological perspectives. Of course, in a slim volume such as this it is impossible to discuss every feminist criminological theory that has emerged over the past 35 years. We explore what we consider to be the major feminist perspectives as well as some spin-offs of these and, at the same time, assess their influence on the discipline of criminology and the practice of criminal justice. In Chapter 5, we reflect on future directions in feminist criminology in light of its historical development and consider its potential for reshaping the discipline as whole. To what extent can feminist criminology contribute to a more progressive criminology? More importantly perhaps, can feminist criminology have a *transformative* impact on "mainstream" criminology, or is it doomed to remain at the margins of the field, or worse still, suffer the fate predicted by Carol Smart (1982) of disappearing into a "theoretical cul-de-sac"? With these pivotal questions in mind, let us undertake a more in-depth examination of feminist criminologies.

2

LIBERAL FEMINIST CRIMINOLOGY

LIBERTY, EQUALITY, SORORITY

As we noted in Chapter 1, one branch of contemporary feminism grew out of various political action organizations formed in the 1960s and early 1970s, whose focus has largely been on lobbying governments to enact legislation giving women the same rights as men. In the United States, these groups include the National Organization for Women (NOW), the Women's Equity Action League (WEAL), and the Congressional Caucus for Women's Issues. Underlying their efforts is the assumption that a primary cause of gender inequality is blocked opportunities due to gender discrimination. Consequently, one of their goals is the passage of legislation outlawing gender discrimination and mandating equal rights for women and men – in employment, education, government, the legal system, and other social institutions. A second goal is to change traditional gender socialization, so that females and males are not instilled with gender stereotyped traits, attitudes, and behaviors, but rather learn to be more alike in how they look, think, and behave. This branch of feminism, which emphasizes "equal rights" and minimizing gender differences, is called *liberal feminism*. In this chapter, we consider the impact of liberal feminism on criminology, beginning with theorizing and research.

CRIME AND THE LIBERATED WOMAN

We have seen that one of the core principles of feminist criminology is the inclusion of women and girls in criminological research. This principle was especially salient in the early development of feminist criminology in the 1970s because prior to this time, women were largely ignored by criminologists who assumed that women simply do not commit crimes. The potential for the study of gender differences in offending to improve our overall understanding of criminal behavior never seemed to occur to criminologists at that time. There were, to be sure, a few books and articles written about "the female offender" before the 1970s (see, for example, Lombroso and Ferrero, 1893; Freud, 1933; Pollak, 1950; Thomas, 1923), but the emphasis of these criminologists was on the anomalous nature of female offending. Women who broke the law were portrayed as physically or psychologically defective at best, as monsters at worst. Their criminality was evidence of their failure as "true" women, for a "true" woman is passive, nurturing, and physically and intellectually weak *by nature*; she is, in other words, what they defined as *feminine*. Therefore, if the female offender was not feminine, she was masculine. In breaking the law, she was behaving not like a woman, but rather like a man.[1] But while these works received some attention when they were published, it was perhaps primarily for their novelty; the criminological community took brief notice, but quickly returned to the important business of studying "real" criminals – i.e. men and boys.

Of course, these criminologists were correct that female arrest and incarceration rates had always been substantially lower than those of males. While the gender gap in offending started to narrow as early as the 1930s, women made up a small percentage of the offender population (Steffensmeier and Cobb, 1981). Moreover, women were typically arrested for public order offenses (e.g. prostitution) and petty theft; they were least likely to be arrested for violent crimes (Smith, 2000). In fact, as one observer noted, women "have had lower rates of crime in *all nations*, in *all communities* within nations, for *all age groups*, for *all periods in recorded history*, and for practically *all crimes*" (Leonard, 1995: 55; author's emphasis). But in the mid-1970s, two criminologists – Freda Adler and Rita

Simon – sounded the alarm that this relatively stable gender gap in criminal offending was changing. Their responses to the questions of how and why fall squarely within a liberal feminist framework, even though they pointed an accusatory finger at feminism for increasing women's participation in crime.

In her book, *Sisters in Crime*, Adler (1975) argued that the United States was experiencing a female crime wave. Men were still committing more crimes than women were, but women's *rate* of offending was rising faster than that of men. For instance, drawing on data from the F.B.I. *Uniform Crime Reports*, Adler reported that between 1960 and 1972, women's arrest rate for robbery increased 277 percent compared with a 169 percent increase for men during the same period. She noted similar changes for juvenile offenders. Thus, it appeared that male and female crime rates were converging, but Adler argued this was so not only in terms of rates, but also with regard to *style*: Women and girls were committing more serious and violent crimes than they had in the past. In short, their criminal behavior was coming to have a striking resemblance to that of men and boys.

Simon (1975), in her book, *Women and Crime*, presented much the same case, although she maintained that the increase in the female crime rate was limited primarily to property offenses. But like Adler, she argued that women's property offenses were becoming more serious and included white-collar and occupational crimes, such as fraud and embezzlement – crimes that historically were the purview of men.

Not surprisingly, the claim that a crime wave was being perpetrated by women and girls in the United States created a buzz not only in academic circles, but also in the popular media. But it was Adler's and Simon's explanation of why this was occurring at that particular time that garnered most attention to their work. Both criminologists identified the "women's liberation movement" as the likely cause of the changes in the frequency and character of female offending.[2] More specifically, they argued that feminism, by opening opportunities to women that had previously been closed to them, also led to their increased participation in crime. "Is it any wonder," Adler (1975: 10) wrote, "that once women were armed with male opportunities they should strive for status, criminal as well as civil, through established male hierarchical channels?" Simon's argument was more nuanced. Her analysis of the crime data indicated that women's violent offending was actually decreasing, which she attributed to their newfound physical, emotional and legal liberation from male control, thereby reducing the feelings of frustration and anger that may cause them to act violently. Nevertheless, as they assumed positions in corporations and government that gave them more power and greater access to money, they were afforded more opportunities – and perhaps were more tempted – to commit certain types of crimes, such as embezzlement and fraud.

Adler's and Simon's explanation for the changes they observed has been called the *emancipation theory* of female offending. Subsequent research to test the theory indicated that their claims were overstated at best. The gender gap in offending was not narrowing as much as they believed; although more women and girls were being arrested and incarcerated than previously – and, as mentioned in Chapters 3 and 4, these trends have continued – they are not women who may be described or who would describe themselves as "liberated."[3] To the contrary, the majority are poor women of color, unemployed, or underemployed, and they were – and are – being arrested and incarcerated largely for relatively minor property crimes, such as shoplifting, passing bad checks, and credit card, loan, or benefits fraud; for prostitution; and for drug offenses. Indeed, one of the major critiques of emancipation theory is that it ignores how the intersecting inequalities of sexism, racism, and classism affect not only criminal offending, but also the policies and practices of the criminal justice system (Chesney-Lind, 2006; Daly, 1989; Leonard, 1982).[4] Empirical tests of emancipation theory have pointed to two alternative explanations for increases in women's arrest and incarceration rates: (1) an increased willingness – some might even argue, zeal – within the criminal justice system to arrest, prosecute, and punish women; and (2) the economic marginalization as well as victimization experiences of some groups of women that put them on specific pathways to offending. We examine both of these explanations more closely in Chapters 3 and 4.

But while Adler's and Simon's work received little empirical support, it is fair to say that it drew more attention – for better and for worse – to female offending than any work that preceded it.[5] As we have noted, much of this attention was a critical response, pointing to the methodological and theoretical weaknesses in both *Sisters in Crime* and *Women and Crime*. Nevertheless, as noted in Chapters 3 and 4, feminist criminologists took up the gauntlet that Adler's and Simon's work symbolically represented and began generating a large body of research that attempted to more accurately and fully capture the experiences of diverse groups of women *and* men with regard to offending, victimization, and criminal justice practice. This does not mean that liberal feminism disappeared from post-1970s criminology. As shown in the remainder of this chapter, it has continued to influence criminological research, education, and practice.

GENDER SOCIALIZATION AND CRIMINAL OFFENDING

Emancipation theory emphasizes changing opportunity structures for women and girls, but other liberal feminist criminologists have focused on how gender socialization may encourage or inhibit criminal offending among females and males. One example of this type of theory is John Hagan's *power-control theory*, which explicitly attempts to explain gender differences in juvenile delinquency. While some (see, for example, Walsh, 2011) have characterized power-control theory as Marxist or as a derivation of conflict theory because it includes an examination of the role of social class as well as gender, we maintain that the theory has much more in common with liberal feminism because it situates the source of gender differences in offending in parents' gender socialization practices.

It is impossible to deny that parents – even those who claim otherwise – socialize their sons and daughters to behave differently. There is abundant empirical evidence indicating that gender socialization begins almost immediately after a child is born, when parents describe and interact with their child differently depending on whether it is a boy or a girl. Parents of boys describe them as big, athletic, active, serious, angry, and determined, whereas parents of girls describe them as small, pretty, delicate, well behaved, emotional, and afraid (Plant *et al.*, 2000; Reid, 1994). These gendered beliefs about children's personalities in turn influence parents' interactions with their children: Parents of boys engage in more physical play with them and encourage their sons to explore more, while parents of girls talk to them more, help them more, and keep them in closer physical proximity (Bronstein, 1988; Burns *et al.*, 1989; MacDonald and Parke, 1986). Hagan (1989; Hagan *et al.*, 1987) observes that this differential gender socialization continues in adolescence, with parents allowing sons greater independence, but imposing greater restrictions on daughters. He also notes, however, that gender socialization differs depending on parents' social class: Lower-class parents tend to socialize their children according to traditional gender norms, whereas middle- and upper-class parents are more flexible in their gender socialization, treating boys and girls similarly.

Power-control theory recognizes that the family, as the first and primary agent of socialization, is a critical institution of social control in any society. At the same time, though, the theory maintains that the way parents exercise this control over their sons and daughters depends to a large extent on family power relations, and family power relations reflect power relations in the workplace. According to Hagan (1989: 13), "work relations structure family relations, particularly relations between fathers and mothers and, in turn, relations between parents and their children, especially mothers and daughters." In others words, the gendered division of power in the home derives from the relative power and command over other resources that fathers and mothers have as a result of the work they do.

Because Hagan is interested in the relative power of fathers and mothers, he focuses on two-parent families and divides them into three possible types: matriarchal, patriarchal, and egalitarian or balanced (McCarthy *et al.*, 1999). A matriarchal family is one in which the wife/mother works outside the home in a position that affords her higher prestige, authority, or income than her husband, thus giving her more power in the family, such as a greater say in decision making. But this type of family is rare – so rare that Hagan and his colleagues (ibid.) were unable to find enough to include in their analysis.[6] Patriarchal families are more common and, according to Hagan, are typical of working-class households. In a traditional patriarchal family, the husband/father is the breadwinner; the wife/mother usually does not work outside the home, so she is responsible for housework and childcare. But even if she does work outside the home, the wife/mother holds a less powerful position than her spouse. In a patriarchal family, then, the husband/father's command of more resources, such as income or authority, at work gives him more power at home, and both spouses accept this gendered division of family power. In fact, they – especially the wife/mother, given her greater responsibility for childcare – reproduce it in the socialization of their children. Daughters in patriarchal families are socialized to be like their mothers – i.e. domestic, restrained, unlikely to take risks – in which case they are unlikely to engage in deviant or delinquent behavior, unless they rebel or try to escape this tight parental control (Hagan, 1990). But sons in patriarchal families come under less parental control, leaving them freer to take risks and to see risk-taking as pleasurable and rewarding. They, therefore, are more likely to participate in deviant or delinquent activities.

Egalitarian or balanced families, according to Hagan, are more common among middle-class and more affluent households. In an egalitarian family, both spouses/parents are likely to work outside the home in positions that afford them relatively equal power and resources, which translates into relatively equal power at home. This equal dominance of spouses/parents results in sons and daughters being treated more alike. Consequently, sons and daughters share similar attitudes – for instance, toward the pleasures and rewards of risk-taking – so their behavior, including their participation in deviant and delinquent activities, will also be similar. It is not that boys' and girls' behavior, deviant or conforming, will be mirror images; as in patriarchal families, boys in egalitarian families are still expected to engage in more delinquency. Nevertheless, power-control theory predicts that the gender gap in deviance and delinquency will be narrower in egalitarian families because, on one hand, girls in these families are encouraged to be independent and to take risks and, on the other hand, boys are encouraged to reject traditional masculine gender norms that support risk-taking and delinquency (McCarthy *et al.*, 1999).

Empirical tests of power-control theory have yielded limited support. For example, most studies show significant sex differences in delinquent and deviant behavior regardless of family type, as well as sex differences in the effectiveness of various types of parental control over children's behavior (Heimer and DeCoster, 1999; Morash and Chesney-Lind, 1991). Moreover, a consistent finding in the research literature is that poverty and economic marginalization, not the freedoms bestowed on youth by middle-class egalitarian socialization practices, significantly increase the probability of delinquent involvement for boys and girls (Heimer and DeCoster, 1999). Although adherence to traditional gender norms appears to lower the risk of delinquency for girls (ibid.), the emphasis in power-control theory on gender *roles* or norms focuses attention on individual factors rather than on social structural causes of both gender inequality and criminal offending. It is the case that social class is related to family structure, but not necessarily in the way depicted by power-control theory. For instance, Hagan focuses on two-parent families, even though the number of single-parent families has grown dramatically over the past four decades (Amato and Maynard, 2007). Most children living in single-parent families (87.5 percent) live with their mother, and single-parent female-headed families are disproportionately represented among the poor (Children's Defense Fund, 2008). It is not difficult to envision how the objective life circumstances of girls and boys growing up in two-parent families in which both parents work are likely to be very different from those of children growing up in single-parent female-headed families, regardless of whether or not their mothers work. And the life circumstances typically engendered by poverty may certainly motivate risk-taking, deviant behavior, and delinquency, independent of parental socialization practices (Chesney-Lind and Shelden, 1992). Hagan and his colleagues (McCarthy *et al.*, 1999) assume that single-parent female-headed families are usually of the matriarchal type, but given the tremendous risk for poverty among these families is it accurate to label them "matriarchal" as defined by power-control theory: having enhanced access to resources through employment, which leads to control at home and freedom from male dominance? Research with poor women heading families alone certainly does not support this conclusion (Edin and Kissane, 2010; Edin and Lein, 1997; Ehrenreich, 2001).

Power-control theory bears an uncanny resemblance to emancipation theory, too, in its argument that children's delinquency, especially the delinquency of daughters, is the result of their mothers' "liberation" through employment that affords these women resources, and hence power, relatively equal to that of their spouses. As Walsh (2011: 35) points out, power-control theory "assumes we can adequately infer the complexity of family dynamics simply by asking about parents' occupations." The theories we will discuss in Chapter 4 attempt to delve more deeply into the relationship between "family dynamics" and gendered differences in both criminal offending and victimization. For now, however, let us continue to examine the influence of liberal feminism in criminology.

WHERE ARE THE WOMEN IN ACADEME?

In Chapter 1, we discussed how, as feminism re-emerged during the 1960s and 1970s, feminist faculty members and students began to scrutinize their campuses and academic departments to identify the myriad ways gender inequality and sexism were reproduced there. In criminology and criminal justice programs, as well as in related disciplines, a glaring manifestation of gender inequality and sexism was the underrepresentation of female faculty and students. If criminology had historically been the study of male offenders, it was also the case that the studying was undertaken mostly by male criminologists. For example, writing in 1997 about the history of women's involvement in the American Society of Criminology (ASC), Freda Adler reported that although the records were spotty, it appeared there were no female members of the ASC from its earliest days (beginning unofficially in 1932 under the leadership of August Vollmer at the University of California, Berkeley) until at least the early 1960s.[7] She points out, for instance, that in 1960, the ASC had 200 members from 14 states and various criminological specialties, but none were women. According to Adler, women began to join the ASC and to attend the annual meetings in the mid-1960s. She attended the meeting in 1967 as a graduate student and noted attendance by a few other female grad students as well as "two very distinguished women colleagues," Eleanor Turo Glueck and Melitta

Schmideberg.[8] Still, there were no women on the meeting program in 1967. In 1972, 11 percent of the ASC's membership – that is, 59 of 529 members – were women; in 1975, 15 percent were women (Adler, 1997). It was also in 1975 that the first paper session solely on women and crime, which was chaired by Freda Adler, was included on the annual meeting program. By 1983, 92 papers on the topic were presented at the annual meeting, and the Division on Women and Crime (DWC), the first division created within the ASC, was approved. The first DWC officers were elected in 1984 (DWC, 2011). Much more information regarding the DWC is discussed in the remaining chapters of this book.

Women's involvement in the ASC likely mirrored their experiences in university criminology departments and the departments of allied disciplines such as sociology, psychology, and political science. There were, first of all, few women in these departments, and the majority of women faculty were concentrated at the lowest academic ranks (Commission on Professionals in Science and Technology, 1987). Of course, the argument could be made that there were few women faculty because so few young women majored in criminology and criminal justice at the undergraduate level. During the 1960s and 1970s, the feminist movement engaged in a variety of efforts to bring more women into higher education and the labor force, particularly in male-dominated fields, and to ensure their equal treatment once they were there. As we mentioned at the outset of this chapter, one liberal feminist strategy to achieve these goals was to enact or change laws so as to provide women and girls with equal educational and employment opportunities. And legislative reform is one of the areas of greatest success for liberal feminism. In the United States, for instance, Title IX of the Education Amendments Act of 1972 forbids sex discrimination in any educational institution that receives federal funding. Executive Order 11246, better known as Affirmative Action, was amended in 1968 to prohibit sex discrimination in addition to discrimination on the basis of race, color, national origin, or religion. Executive Order 11246 applies to employers who hold contracts with the federal government, which includes most colleges and universities, and requires these employers to take affirmative steps to recruit, train, and promote women and racial and ethnic minorities. Title VII of the 1964 Civil Rights Act forbids discrimination in hiring, benefits, and other personnel decisions such as promotions, on the basis of sex as well as race, color, national origin, or religion, by employers of 15 or more employees. And the Equal Employment Opportunity Act (EEOA) of 1972 amended the Civil Rights Act to include public employees and to further establish affirmative employment measures.

There is no doubt that laws such as these benefited countless women. The number of women attending college and graduate school increased dramatically during the 1960s and 1970s. In the U.S. in 1960, for example, women were 36 percent of undergraduates and 35 percent of bachelor's degree recipients. By 1970, these numbers had increased to 41 percent of undergraduates and 41 percent of bachelor's degree recipients; and by 1980, women outnumbered men as undergraduate students (52.3 percent), a phenomenon that continues today, and earned 47.3 percent of bachelor's degrees. The percentage of female master's degree recipients also rose during the period 1960–1980 (from 32 percent to 49.3 percent), but the percentage of female doctorates during this time, while significantly improving, remained relatively low: 10 percent in 1960, 13 percent in 1970, and 29.8 percent in 1980 (still less than one-third of all doctoral recipients) (Renzetti and Curran, 1989). Unfortunately, comparable data are not available for degree recipients in criminology and criminal justice specifically; they are available for psychology and for the broader study area of social sciences, which includes criminology as well as sociology and political science – departments that often house criminology and criminal justice programs or whose undergraduate students subsequently pursue graduate study in criminology or criminal justice. As Table 2.1 shows, the percentage of women degree recipients in these fields increased steadily and significantly at the undergraduate and graduate levels.

Certainly, these data may be taken as an indication that feminist efforts to bring more women into the academy, as well as into traditionally male-dominated fields such as criminology, were successful. There is also evidence, however, that while legislation prohibited overt forms of discrimination, female students and faculty routinely encountered subtle and, in some cases, not-so-subtle discrimination. Research in the 1980s by the Association

Table 2.1 Degrees earned by women in psychology and the social sciences, 1970–80

	Psychology								
	Bachelor's degrees			Master's degrees			Doctoral degrees		
Year	Total	# to Women	% to Women	Total	# to Women	% to Women	Total	# to Women	% to Women
1970–71	38,187	21,227	44.4	5,717	2,322	40.6	2,144	515	24.0
1975–76	50,278	27,380	54.5	10,167	5,031	49.5	3,157	1,042	33.0
1980–81	41,068	26,736	65.1	10,223	6,157	60.2	3,576	1,574	44.0
	Social Sciences[1]								
	Bachelor's degrees			Master's degrees			Doctoral degrees		
Year	Total	# to Women	% to Women	Total	# to Women	% to Women	Total	# to Women	% to Women
1970–71	155,324	57,151	36.8	16,539	4,706	28.5	3,660	507	13.9
1975–76	126,396	47,705	37.7	15,953	5,039	31.6	4,157	895	21.5
1980–81	100,513	44,382	44.1	11,945	4,488	41.9	3,122	848	27.2

[1]Includes degrees in social sciences, general; anthropology; archeology; criminology; demography and population affairs; economics; geography; history; international relations and affairs; political science and government; sociology; urban affairs/studies; and social sciences and history, other.

Source: U.S. Department of Education, National Center for Education Statistics, *Digest of Education Statistics, 1995*, Tables 285 and 287. Retrieved from http://nces.ed.gov.

of American Colleges and Universities (AACU), for instance, found that female undergraduate and graduate students, especially those in courses and programs of study that were male-dominated, encountered more than 35 different forms of sex discrimination, which they termed "micro-inequities" because of the subtle, everyday character of the behaviors. Among the most common micro-inequities they discovered were male students being called on more frequently in class; references to males as "men," but to females as "girls" or "gals"; and disparaging remarks about women's intellectual abilities or academic commitment (e.g. "This may be a little too complicated for you girls to understand.") (Hall and Sandler, 1985; Sandler and Hall, 1986). Female faculty, too, encountered similar micro-inequities: male colleagues and even students felt free to address them as "honey" or "dear," or they were called "Miss" or "Mrs." while their male colleagues were referred to as "Dr."; they were expected to record the minutes at department meetings or as the lone woman on a committee to provide the "women's perspective," as if one woman could speak for all; their personal lives were scrutinized; and comments were made about their appearance or physical attributes (e.g. "With legs like those, you should wear skirts more often.") (Sandler and Hall, 1986).

This latter example highlights another frequent and serious form of discrimination that many female students and faculty encountered in the academy: sexual harassment. Researchers report that although sexual harassment occurs in all types of occupations, it is especially pervasive in a male-dominated workplace (Gruber and Morgan, 2005). Not surprisingly, then, researchers in the 1980s found that for women in criminology and criminal justice programs, sexual harassment and intimidation were not uncommon experiences. Betsy Stanko (1992) surveyed members of the Division on Women and Crime of the ASC and found that the majority of respondents (59 percent) had been sexually harassed in graduate school by a faculty member or another student, and nearly one-third (31 percent) had been sexually harassed while conducting research or fieldwork. In most cases, the harassment took the form of sexual or suggestive comments, but sometimes involved unwanted touching, and several respondents reported being physically assaulted.

As Stanko (ibid.) rightly argued, sexual harassment contributes to women's marginalization in the academy, and she recommended that faculty members incorporate into class discussions strategies for handling sexism and sexual harassment and make issues of sexual safety part of the criminology/criminal justice curriculum. Curriculum reform, in fact, was another major feminist strategy for improving the status and success of women in criminology and criminal justice. Liberal feminists, in particular, have long had faith in education as a means to resocialize men and women to accept less traditional gender roles. Beginning in the 1970s, then, many criminology and criminal justice programs added courses on "women's issues" to their offerings. These have often been referred to as the "Women-in" and "Women-and" courses (e.g. Women in Criminal Justice, Women and Crime) or as the "Add women and stir" approach to curriculum reform (McIntosh, 1983). But as Lynne Goodstein (1992) has pointed out, these courses often did little more than reinforce gender stereotypes. The courses were typically taught by women to primarily women students, and were quickly marginalized and devalued in many departments. Efforts to revise the curriculum so that feminist scholarship and gender were integrated into *all* criminology and criminal justice courses were strongly resisted or were rejected outright (Garrison *et al*., 1992).[9] Consequently, the majority of criminology and criminal justice courses well into the 1980s continued to focus on the behavior of men, and the popular textbooks for these courses reinforced the notion that crime and the study of it are the purview of men (Dorworth and Henry, 1992; Mahan and Anthony, 1992; Wright, 1992).

WHERE ARE THE WOMEN IN THE CRIMINAL JUSTICE PROFESSIONS?

The impact of legislative reforms such as Title VII, the EEOA, and Affirmative Action in the U.S., as well as the 1975 Sex Discrimination Act in Great Britain, can also be seen in changes in the sex composition of various criminal justice professions from the 1960s to the 1980s. Successful lawsuits challenging hiring and employment policies and practices that unfairly disadvantage women forced changes in police departments and other law enforcement agencies, correctional facilities, and law firms.[10] Consequently, more women became police officers, correctional officers, lawyers, and judges. Consider, for example, that it was not until 1968 that female police officers in an American municipality were assigned to patrol duties: Betty Blankenship and Elizabeth Coffal of the Indianapolis, Indiana police department were the first female police officers in the United States "to wear a patrol officer's uniform, strap a gun belt to their waists, drive a marked patrol car, and answer general police calls for service," just as male officers did (Morash *et al.*, 2006: 215). In 1971, there were still only seven female police officers on patrol in the United States (Gates, 1976). Most women police officers were assigned specialized work, processing cases involving women and children – a role that was viewed within departments as more akin to social work than crime fighting (Morash *et al.*, 2006).[11] In 1975, women were 2.2 percent of sworn municipal police personnel in the U.S.; by 1985, their representation on municipal police forces had grown to 6.8 percent. Although this latter figure represents more than a 300 percent increase in female officers in 10 years, women continued to be underrepresented in policing, especially in the supervisory or command ranks, not only in the U.S., but also in Great Britain (Farrell, 2000; Heidensohn, 2000). Notably, the majority of large police departments that had the highest percentages of female officers in the 1990s were at that time or had previously been under consent decrees in which they agreed to hire and promote more women (and often minorities) within a specified period of time (Gilbert, 2000; Scarborough, 2000).

Women in the U.S. were less successful in joining state-level police agencies; by the end of the 1990s, only 5.2 percent of state troopers in the U.S. were women (Meloy, 2000). At the federal level, women's representation among officers with arrest and firearms authority varied dramatically, with the lowest percentages in the Drug Enforcement Administration (DEA) and the Secret Service, and the highest percentage in the Internal Revenue Service (IRS) (ibid.). The number of female correctional officers also remained fairly low, despite increased employment. Historically, female correctional officers worked only in women's facilities or in the small, segregated women's sections of male facilities. In the 1970s, women in the U.S. began to be hired as officers in male facilities, again largely as the result of successful lawsuits (Stohr, 2006). Between 1978 and 1988, the number of women working as correctional officers in men's facilities grew by more than 200 percent, so that by 1988 women were 13 percent of correctional officers in American men's prisons (Morton, 1991). In Canada, by 1984, women were 10 percent of correctional officers in Canadian federal prisons (Zupan, 1992).

Women's most dramatic increases in criminal justice employment were in the field of law. At the start of the 1960s, women were 3 percent of lawyers in the U.S., but by the end of the 1970s, they were 14 percent of lawyers in this country. During the same period in Canada, the percentage of female attorneys increased from 3 percent to 15 percent (Hagan and Kay, 1995). Belknap (2001) reports that in England, women were 10 percent of attorneys in 1971, but by the close of the 1980s they were entering the profession in rates equal to men.[12] Interestingly, though, Siemsen (2006) correlates the increase in the number of female lawyers, at least in the U.S., with the increase in legal aid societies and government public defenders' offices throughout the country. The number of these types of law offices grew quickly following the 1963 case of *Gideon v. Wainwright*, in which the Supreme Court ruled that indigent defendants being tried on felony charges had the right to legal counsel and if they could not afford a lawyer, the government would provide one free of charge. Nine years later, in *Argersinger v. Hamlin* (1972), the Court extended the right to counsel to defendants in misdemeanor cases if they faced a possible jail sentence. Of course, public defenders and legal aid attorneys have relatively low prestige compared with other attorneys and are among the lowest paid.

This last observation returns us to a point raised regarding the increase in female faculty and students in criminology and criminal justice. As Schulz (2000: 179) phrased it, "Legal equality has been achieved, but whether actual equality exists is open to question." Indeed, a large body of research over the past three decades has documented numerous obstacles to gender equality that women in all criminal justice professions continue to confront. These include: overt opposition from male co-workers, who see the inclusion of women as a threat to the prestige of the occupation or to the masculinity attached to it – or to them as individual men; persistent gender stereotypes about women being weak, overly emotional, vain, or seductive – traits that not only inhibit women's ability to fight crime and effectively control prisoners, but that also endanger their male co-workers; lack of mentoring by senior co-workers; and sexual harassment (American Bar Association, 2001; Collins, 2006; Horne, 2006; Jurik and Martin, 2001; Stohr, 2006). Thus, like their sisters in the academy, women in the criminal justice professions continued to experience overt and more subtle forms of gender-based discrimination and harassment despite legal reforms intended to remedy these problems.

THE LIBERAL FEMINIST LEGACY

It is somewhat ironic that liberal feminist theories blame women's increasing equality with men for changes in female offending, given that a major goal of liberal feminists is to promote gender equality through legislative reform and resocialization toward the adoption of non-traditional gender roles for women and men. In this chapter, we examined two popular liberal feminist theories of female offending, and we discussed how various laws prohibiting sex discrimination and promoting equal opportunities in education and employment have helped bring more women into criminology and criminal justice as students, faculty, and criminal justice professionals. We have also noted, however, that many feminist criminologists have critiqued liberal feminist theories on methodological grounds and for other significant limitations, including the theories' lack of attention to how gender inequality *intersects* with racial, ethnic, social class, and other inequalities to influence particular outcomes for different groups of women and men. These feminist criminologists posit alternative explanations for gender differences in offending as well as in educational outcomes and success in the criminal justice professions. Moreover, while these feminist criminologists recognize the importance of legislation and law suits to promote – some might even say, force – changes in educational and occupational opportunities for women, they emphasize that such strategies are typically insufficient to bring about and ensure not only gender equity, but also equity for racial and ethnic minorities, the poor, lesbians and gay men, and other groups that experience widespread institutionalized discrimination. It is to these alternative theories and social change strategies that we turn our attention in subsequent chapters.

3

THE SUBORDINATION OF WOMEN

MARXIST, RADICAL, AND SOCIALIST FEMINIST CRIMINOLOGIES

As we noted in Chapter 1, around the same time that liberal feminism was developing, a second, more radical feminist perspective emerged as well. This brand of feminism grew out of the politically left-wing social movements of the 1960s and 1970s, including the anti-war, Civil Rights, and anti-colonialism movements. Women who were active in these movements often felt marginalized by male leaders who relegated them to traditional "women's roles" (Evans, 1979; Rosen, 2000). In response, women formed their own activist groups, centered on achieving equality for women. But while they supported liberal feminist efforts to bring about change by lobbying for passage of various legislative reforms, these feminists, with roots in leftist politics, questioned whether gender equality was possible in a social system – capitalism – built fundamentally on inequality.

The social unrest of the "turbulent 1960s" was mirrored in many academic departments on college and university campuses around the world. In criminology, a number of theoretical approaches grew in popularity as faculty and students took to the tasks of questioning authority and challenging the status quo. *Labeling theory*, for example, developed in rebellion against the long-held *absolutist* assumption in criminology that crime is behavior that violates a law; a law is a rule that is consensually agreed upon by the members of a society. In other words, criminologists had traditionally assumed that there are some behaviors that are inherently criminal. Therefore, the criminologist's job is to identify those who break the law and figure out what it is about them (e.g. their physical or psychological make-up) or about their environment (e.g. living in socially disorganized neighborhoods) that causes them to commit crimes. In contrast, labeling theorists took a *relativist* stance on crime, arguing that a behavior (or an attribute, or even an idea) becomes criminal or deviant only when it is defined as such by a group of observers. Nothing, then, is inherently criminal or deviant; it becomes criminal or deviant when it is labeled as such: "The deviant is one to whom that label has been successfully applied; deviant behavior is behavior that people so label" (Becker, 1973: 9).

Elaborating on this bold assertion, labeling theorists argued that what is labeled criminal or deviant *depends* on several factors such as situational and historical contexts; the characteristics of the individual engaged in the behavior, espousing the idea, or displaying the attribute in question; and the characteristics of the definers. For example, if a man forces a woman to have sex against her will, most people would define that act as rape. However, historically if the man was the woman's husband, such an act was not defined in law, by the general public, by the man himself, and perhaps by the woman as rape; instead, it was seen as his marital "right" and her marital "duty." For labeling theorists, then, crime and deviance are products of social *interaction*: It is less important that an individual violates a law or a rule than it is that others respond to that individual by labeling him or her a criminal or deviant. This response may be informal (e.g. refusing to socialize with the labeled individual), but labeling theorists were more interested in formal, public responses – what they called *status degradation ceremonies* – because these typically cause the labeled individual to undergo a fundamental change in identity: They *become* what they have been labeled and begin to behave in ways that conform to stereotypes or preconceived notions of how someone "like them" acts, thinks, and looks. The labeled individual has no choice but to then embark on a *deviant career* (Cohen, 1966).

Labeling theorists were also quick to point out that the relative power or powerlessness of an individual or group affects their ability to successfully attach a criminal or deviant label to someone or something and to avoid being labeled criminal or deviant themselves (Becker, 1970). Given the power imbalance between women and men in most societies, one might assume that labeling theory would be applicable to the study of gender and crime. One prominent labeling theorist, Edwin Schur (1984: 3–4), who examined the process by which women are labeled "deviant," pointed out:

> in our society being treated as deviant has been a standard feature of life as a female. With great regularity women have been labeled – and they are still being labeled – "aggressive," "bitchy," "hysterical," "fat," "homely," "masculine," and "promiscuous." Judgments such as these, and the social reactions that accompany them, represent a very potent kind of deviance-defining. They may not put the presumed "offender" in jail, but they do typically damage her reputation, induce shame, and lower her "life chances." These informal ways of defining and reacting to women should be of great interest to the sociologist. They help us recognize perceptions and ideas that frequently dominate interactions between males and females. They also show how such daily interaction reflects, and in turn reinforces, the overall disparities in social and economic power between the sexes.

Schur went on to empirically demonstrate gender differences in what gets labeled deviant and how these labels differentially impact women and men. But despite his exhortation to his colleagues to pay attention to gendered labeling and its consequences, most labeling theorists focused solely on men and boys, and if women were included, they were portrayed far less sympathetically or as peripheral to the "real action" (Naffine, 1996).[1] At the same time, other criminologists were critical of labeling theory for not going far enough, in their view, in examining "the way in which deviance and criminality are shaped by society's larger structure of power and institutions" (Taylor *et al.*, 1973: 169). These criminologists questioned the legitimacy of the legal system itself and regarded traditional, "establishment" criminologists as "defenders of the status quo": pro-government, pro-industry, legitimating oppression, "scholarship in the service of social control" (Quinney, 1973: 26). They undertook the development of what they considered a "new" criminology – a criminology grounded in Marxist theory that explained crime and the treatment of offenders largely in terms of the social class inequality inherent in contemporary capitalism. It was from – or, some may argue, in response to – this new or *critical criminology* that Marxist feminist, radical feminist, and socialist feminist criminologies emerged. The remainder of this chapter examines each of these perspectives in turn, and then discusses their impact on criminology and criminal justice.

MARXIST FEMINIST CRIMINOLOGY

Karl Marx actually had very little to say about crime or criminals, and some of what he said was rather unforgiving.[2] But to the pioneers of critical criminology, Marx's analysis of social class relations under capitalism was foundational. More specifically, critical criminologists argued that in capitalist societies, such as the United States and Great Britain, all social life and interaction can be understood in terms of the class structure, a structure divided between those who own and control the means of production (i.e. a small, cohesive group of wealthy and powerful men) and those who are subordinate to them (i.e. the majority of the population: those who own relatively little and must sell their labor in exchange for wages). The law and the criminal justice system, like other social institutions in capitalist societies, reflect this class division. If one looks at who gets arrested, who appears in the criminal courts, and who makes up the vast majority of jail and prison inmates, one will find predominantly poor and working class people. It's not that the poor and working class commit more crimes. It is that much of what the wealthy do is not defined as criminal; in fact, their actions may even be regarded as savvy business practices (Krisberg, 1975). If the wealthy are apprehended for breaking a law, they have the resources to successfully defend themselves and avoid prosecution or severe punishment. Consequently, critical criminologists gave considerable attention to documenting both "crimes of the powerful" (e.g. white collar crime, state crime, human rights violations) and the biased operation of the criminal justice system in favor of the economically privileged and against the poor and other oppressed groups, including racial and ethnic minorities (see, for example, Lynch and Groves, 1986; Pearce, 1976; Reiman, 1979).

Conspicuously absent from the writing of most critical criminologists, however, was an analysis of gender. For instance, in *The New Criminology*, considered by many to be the ground-breaking book in critical criminology, authors Taylor *et al.*, (1973) completely overlooked the relevance of gender or the need to explain offending by women and girls. Moreover, the women's movement was raising awareness of the gendered nature of criminal victimization and the vulnerability of women and girls to specific crimes such as sexual assault and domestic violence, crimes also largely ignored by critical criminologists (Gelsthorpe and Morris, 1988; Klein and Kress, 1976; Naffine, 1996). To rectify these deficiencies, some women criminologists – and some men, too – took up the Marxist analysis of crime, but drew on Marx and Engels' writings about women and the family under capitalism to explain female offending and victimization. This theoretical perspective is known as *Marxist feminist criminology*.

Marxist feminist criminologists begin with the premise that the social class relations of capitalism are the primary cause of women's oppression. Capitalism fundamentally altered relations in the family by moving production out of the home and into the public sphere. Men went off to work, while women remained at home to care for children. But while men earn wages, no matter how meager, women's household labor is unpaid; it is reproductive, not productive labor and, therefore, it is devalued (Maidment, 2006). The economic marginalization of women and, consequently, their subordination to men are reflected in the types of crimes women commit as well as their victimization experiences. For example, Marxist feminist criminologists pointed out that while women's violent offending was not increasing the way Adler (1975) and Simon (1975) had claimed it was, women were nevertheless committing more property crimes, including larceny-theft, fraud, and forgery. Examined more closely, these were crimes women had traditionally committed: shoplifting, writing bad checks, credit card fraud, and welfare fraud – crimes congruent with their traditional roles as homemakers, caregivers, and consumers (Steffensmeier, 1978, 1982). In contrast to Adler and Simon, these criminologists explained changes in women's property offending as a direct outcome of their increasing economic marginalization and the "feminization of poverty" (Box, 1987; Chesney-Lind, 1986; Daly, 1989). Data show, in fact, that women, especially women of color, are disproportionately represented among the poor, and that the poverty rate of single-parent female-headed households is more than twice the poverty rate of single-parent male-headed households (Renzetti *et al.*, 2012). As Chesney-Lind (1997) has pointed out, the typical female offender is young, non-white, a high school drop-out, a single mother, and poor.

Similarly, Marxist feminist criminologists explained women's vulnerability to certain types of criminal victimization in terms of class inequality under capitalism. Julia and Herman Schwendinger (1983), for example, argue that violent crimes against women, such as rape, are not widespread across all societies and in all historical periods. Rather, modern capitalist societies have particularly high rates of rape and other forms of violence against women because the male dominance that breeds male violence is a result of the exploitative class relations inherent in modern capitalism. Therefore, from a Marxist feminist perspective, the solution to the crime problem – female *and* male offending *and* victimization – is the demise of capitalism and its replacement by a more egalitarian economic system in which women along with men are fairly paid, productive workers; housework and childcare are socialized; and marriage and sexual relationships do not mimic private property relations (Daly and Chesney-Lind, 1988; Maidment, 2006; Schwendinger and Schwendinger, 1983).

Some feminists, though, were critical of the Marxist feminist perspective, arguing that Marxist feminists' emphasis on class oppression was misplaced. After all, in socialist societies in Latin America and Eastern Europe one continued to find patriarchy alive and well. Women in these countries did not appear "liberated;" they appeared exhausted from the "double shift" of a full-time job in the paid labor force and primary responsibility for housework and childcare as well (see, for instance, Scott, 1974). And there was no indication that intimate partner violence, sexual assault, and other types of gender-based violence had been eradicated in these societies. Alternative feminist perspectives, including radical feminist criminology and socialist feminist criminology, attempt to redress the weaknesses in Marxist feminist criminology.

RADICAL FEMINIST CRIMINOLOGY

Radical feminist criminology begins with the assumption that gender inequality or sexism, not social class inequality, is the most fundamental form of oppression. It is patriarchy, not capitalism, that is the "enemy," because, according to radical feminists, women historically were the first oppressed social group, and today women continue to be the most oppressed social group in the world, regardless of whether the society one examines is capitalist or socialist. No matter what their social class, their race or their ethnicity, men enjoy gender privilege at the expense of women. The chief means by which men maintain their gender privilege and dominance is through control of women's sexuality. More specifically, radical feminists argue that male power and female subordination are preserved through *compulsory heterosexuality* and the threat or actual use of *violence* (MacKinnon, 1989; Walby, 1990). Pornography, rape, sexual harassment, battering, and other types of physical, psychological, and sexual abuse all serve to keep men and women in their respective places – i.e. to keep men in power and to keep women powerless (MacKinnon, 1989; Stanko, 1986).

Remedying this fundamental problem, then, requires significantly greater social change than simply enacting laws to prohibit sex discrimination, as liberal feminists try to do. From the radical feminist perspective, all social institutions in a patriarchal society, including the criminal justice system, are male dominated and serve to reflect and preserve men's interests. To trust that such institutions as they are currently structured could bring about meaningful change on women's behalf is considered naïve at best (MacKinnon, 1989; Radford, 1987). Even the overthrow of capitalism, as Marxist feminists advocate, is not sufficient from a radical feminist perspective, since it is patriarchal relations, not class relations, that must be destroyed (Daly and Chesney-Lind, 1988).

In criminology, radical feminists focused less on women as offenders than on women as victims. Radical feminist criminologists have been among the leading researchers studying the causes and consequences of violence against women and the failure of the criminal justice system to protect women from men's violence. Research by radical feminist criminologists has been instrumental in drawing attention to the fact that perpetration of and victimization by violent crime is gendered. Men are more likely than women to both perpetrate violent crime and to be victimized by it, but research by radical feminist criminologists and others has consistently documented the alarming frequency of violence against women throughout the world and the multitude of forms it takes, including sexual harassment, sexual assault and rape, battering, and femicide (see Renzetti *et al.*, 2011). Moreover, while girls and women are routinely given advice about keeping themselves safe – e.g. don't talk to strangers, don't go out alone at night – research shows that they are significantly more likely to be harmed by someone they know in their own homes than by a stranger on the street or in an alley (Stanko, 1996, 2001).[3] Radical feminist criminologists further pointed out that despite the pervasiveness of violence against women, the police, the courts, and criminologists of various theoretical persuasions have nonetheless been preoccupied with other types of male crime, especially male-on-male street crime. At the same time, radical feminist criminological research has brought to light the abysmal failure of the criminal justice system in responding to women and girls who have been victimized, and in holding men and boys accountable for the violence they perpetrate against them. Radical feminists, for example, presented abundant data showing how when a woman is raped, it is she, not the rapist, who typically must prove her innocence by convincing criminal justice personnel and others that she conforms to traditional standards of respectable femininity and that she did nothing to precipitate the rape (e.g. she was not drinking or using drugs, did not willingly go with the assailant or invite him to her home, did not dress or behave seductively, did not have a previous intimate relationship with him) (see Caringella, 2008; Estrich, 1988; see also "Nature of Clothing," 1990; "New Zealand Judge," 1996). Similarly, radical feminists documented the unresponsiveness of the criminal justice system to battered women's calls for help, sometimes resulting in the women's deaths (Hague and Malos, 1993; Radford and Russell, 1992; Schechter, 1982).

Indeed, perhaps the greatest contribution of radical feminist criminology has been its unrelenting effort to turn the professional and public spotlights on men's violence against women and the dangerous consequences that a patriarchal criminal justice system has for female victims. But this is also the source of much of the criticism that has been leveled against radical feminist criminology, including criticisms from other feminists. For instance, some feminists have criticized radical feminist criminology for its cynicism toward the criminal justice system. While radical feminist criminologists certainly have good reason to call the legal system to task for its repeated failure to protect women and girls from men's violence and its sexist treatment of female victims of gender-based crime, it is somewhat simplistic to portray the system as purely an instrument of male domination and to abandon any hope of reforming the system so that it is more effective in its responses (Messerschmidt, 1993). As we discuss later, significant changes have occurred in recent years that have measurably improved police and court responses to female victims of male violence.

A related criticism has focused on radical feminist criminology's characterization of *all* men as dominant and oppressive, and *all* women as subordinated and victimized. As some observers point out, there have been pro-feminist men working for gender equality and an end to violence, including violence against women, since the resurgence of feminism in the 1960s and 1970s, and their numbers have grown over the years (DeKeseredy, 2000; Lorber, 2009; Tolman and Edleson, 2011). And while all men may enjoy some gender privilege, many men are dominated and oppressed by other, more powerful men, who exercise other types of privilege such as class and race privilege. Similarly, likelihood of violent victimization is not shared equally by all women; some groups of women, especially women who are poor, are at greater risk of violent victimization (Renzetti, 2011a; Richie, 2012). In short, by giving gender oppression primacy over other forms of oppression, radical feminist criminology downplays the salience of other inequalities, particularly classism and racism, in women's – and men's – lives.

Radical feminist criminology has clearly had a major impact on services for female victims of gender-based violence and on criminal justice practice with regard to these crimes, a point to which we will return momentarily. First, however, we turn our attention to another feminist criminological perspective that has sometimes been characterized as an attempt to "marry" Marxist feminism with radical feminism.

SOCIALIST FEMINIST CRIMINOLOGY

Socialist feminist criminologists are concerned with the ways in which capitalism and patriarchy converge to produce gender differences in offending and victimization, as well as the differential ways the criminal justice system treats females and males. In other words, socialist feminist criminologists do not foreground social class inequality *or* gender inequality, but rather examine how social class inequality *and* gender inequality operate together to affect the crimes women and men commit and the crimes committed against them along with the criminal justice system's responses to gendered offending and victimization. From this perspective, the State (i.e. government at all levels) is a key player in linking capitalism and patriarchy. As Nancy Jurik (1999: 43) explains, "the State is seldom a neutral mediator or protector of women, nor is it merely a disseminator of the 'people's will.'" The State in its capacity to enact and enforce law has tremendous power to reinforce (or undermine) capitalism and patriarchy (see also Carlen, 1988; Davis, 1993).

James Messerschmidt (1986, 1993) is widely recognized for his articulation of socialist feminist criminology, and his work served as a springboard for much subsequent socialist feminist criminological research. Messerschmidt maintained that an understanding of women's and men's crime requires an analysis of gender socialization and the gendered division of labor at home and in the workplace. For instance, Messerschmidt points out that wealthy men who hold powerful positions in government and the economy are ideally situated to commit very serious and harmful crimes, in terms of both the harm they cause and the losses they incur – crimes such as insider stock trading, fraudulent investment schemes, sale of products known to be hazardous or potentially lethal, illegal disposal of toxic waste, and human rights violations.[4] The workplace socialization at this elite level reinforces earlier gender socialization into masculinity that emphasized material success, competitiveness, risk-taking, and winning at all costs. Among the corporate male elite, ethics and morality must sometimes be sidestepped for the "greater good" of the corporation or government. Thus, increasing or maintaining profitability, remaining competitive in the marketplace, or preserving national security may all mean one must occasionally disregard, "bend," or "wink at" the law (see, for example, Messerschmidt, 1995).

Working-class and poor men simply do not have the opportunities to commit corporate and political crimes, but they do have ample opportunities to engage in traditional street crime, such as theft and fencing stolen goods, drug dealing, assault, and robbery. But, as Messerschmidt (1993) points out, these crimes reflect not only their social class position in a capitalist society, but also their access to activities that are largely gender-segregated and that are expressions of their socialized conceptions of masculinity.

This same classed and gendered social system excludes most women from the suites of power where they would be afforded opportunities to commit serious corporate and governmental crimes.[5] Moreover, feminine socialization as well as the greater supervision and control to which females are subjected by their parents and other relatives, teachers, boyfriends, and husbands, result in far fewer opportunities for them to commit other types of crimes too, and to some extent inhibits their motivation to offend. Although Messerschmidt's work has largely focused on masculinities as central to understanding crime because males of all social classes commit more crimes than females, his socialist feminist analysis applies to female offending in that he points out how women's and girls' socialized conceptions of femininity and their social and economic positions in society not only reduce their likelihood of engaging in crime, but also affect the types of crimes they commit and the way they commit these crimes when they do offend. Similar to Marxist feminists, socialist feminists connect female offending to the economic marginalization of women and girls, showing that female offending is made up primarily of larceny theft, minor fraud and embezzlement, street hustling, and drug offenses (Gilfus, 1993; Messerschmidt, 1986; Miller, 1986).[6] But even when women commit crimes traditionally dominated by men, their offending is shaped by feminine gender ideologies. In Miller's (1998) study of robbery, for instance, she found that men typically use guns, physical contact, and violence in male-on-male robberies – techniques that we associate with masculinity. Women, in contrast, usually rob other women, whom they consider vulnerable and easy to intimidate. If women do rob men, they play on gender stereotypes of women as weak and sexually available so as to manipulate their targets into situations in which the robbery is more easily accomplished.

We have noted that the greater control to which girls and women are subjected by parents, boyfriends, and husbands may reduce their opportunities to engage in crime, but at the same time, some socialist feminist criminologists have considered how this control may contribute to female offending (Brown *et al.*, 2007). These socialist feminist criminologists maintain that control of girls and women may not be benevolent, but is instead abusive, and they examine links between female victimization and offending. Chesney-Lind (1997), for example, studied young women who get caught up in the juvenile justice system as runaways and discovered that many leave home to escape physical and sexual abuse (see also Davis, 1993). Additional research shows that system-involved girls are more likely than system-involved boys to have been abused (Flynn *et al.*, 2007; Siegel and Williams, 2003; Widom and Maxfield, 2001). Socialist feminist analyses, then, challenge the traditional notions of home as a "safe haven" and the legal system as "protector" of women and girls (Jurik, 1999), a point we will discuss further in the next section of this chapter.

In summary, socialist feminist criminologists emphasize the dual importance and interactive effects of social class and gender inequalities in shaping females' and males' offending as well as their victimization experiences. Socialist feminist criminologists also challenge traditional depictions of the criminal justice system as a value-neutral protector acting in citizens' "best interests," regardless of their social class or gender. But despite the strengths of this perspective, socialist feminist criminology has been criticized on several grounds, perhaps the most important of which is the tendency to overlook the tremendous diversity of experience across groups of women and men who differ not only in terms of social class, but also by race and ethnicity, nationality, sexual orientation, age, and physical ability. The socialist feminist analysis of men's domination and women's oppression is based largely on studies of contemporary Western industrial societies – and a limited number of communities within those societies at that – which means that significant historical and cross-cultural differences in gender relations are missed (Messerschmidt, 1993). "Too often patriarchy is portrayed as a universal, invariant, and total system of male domination over women" (Jurik, 1999: 44). Black feminists, in particular, have pointed out that socialist feminist criminology failed to fully examine racism as a system of oppression of women *and* men (Rice, 1990). Although racism was acknowledged by socialist feminists, it was not systematically integrated into their analyses and remained peripheral at best. Rice (ibid.), for instance, is critical of socialist (and other) feminist criminologies for universalizing white women's experiences, and she calls for an analysis of the *simultaneous* influences of gender, class, *and race* – or what others refer to as the "multiple axes of oppression" (Risman, 2004) – on women's and men's offending, victimization, and interactions with the criminal justice system (see also Richie, 1996). This critique has important implications for social change as well, for as some critics point out, eliminating patriarchy and capitalism will not inevitably result in a more egalitarian or just society if other forms of oppression, such as racism, remain intact.

Although socialist feminist criminologists have responded to these critiques by incorporating an examination of multiple inequalities into their work, it has been black feminist criminologists who have developed this analysis most extensively. We discuss black feminist criminology in Chapter 4. For now, however, let us consider the impact of Marxist, radical, and socialist feminist criminologies on the criminal justice system.

THE VICTIMIZATION – AND REVICTIMIZATION – OF WOMEN

As discussed previously, among the most significant contributions of Marxist, socialist, and especially radical feminist criminologists has been documenting the pervasiveness and serious nature of violence against women and, simultaneously, the ineffective or, worse, detrimental responses of the criminal legal system to women's victimization, what came to be known as the *second* victimization. But these feminists did not just describe the injustices; they mobilized to bring about change. One outcome of this feminist social activism was the creation of special services and safe spaces for female victims of male violence: e.g. sexual assault hotlines and crisis centers, Sexual Assault Nurse Examiner (SANE) programs,[7] domestic violence coalitions, and residential shelters for battered women to escape their abusers. Initially, at least, many of these services were established for women by women – many of whom had themselves been the victims of male violence. The services were founded on the principles of women's rights to bodily integrity and self-determination, and they were organized in egalitarian and non-hierarchical ways (Goodmark, 2012). Chief among their goals was – and, for most, continues to be – support for and empowerment of victimized women by providing them with assistance in navigating the legal system and various social services (e.g. health care, education, housing, and welfare). Educational campaigns were also mounted, designed to raise awareness about the problem of violence against women, to change attitudes and behaviors toward both victims and perpetrators, and to let victims know that they are not alone and help is available. These educational campaigns have taken many forms, from public service announcements, posters, and billboards, to Take Back the Night marches, to training curricula for professionals.[8] Regardless of the actual words or images used, however, an underlying, unifying theme was to "break the silence" surrounding violence against women.

A companion theme to breaking the silence was *perpetrator accountability*. Legal scholar Leigh Goodmark (2012: 2) notes that despite many feminists' critiques of the legal system as a tool of male domination, they were "surprisingly willing to rely on the law and on the men charged with enforcing the law – police, prosecutors, lawyers, and judges – to protect women from societal expressions of male domination." Feminist activists argued that men assaulted and abused women because they could get away with it, and they demanded that these acts should be "criminalized."

Of course, rape was a crime and it carried severe sanctions, but, as we noted earlier, unless the act in question met a narrow set of criteria (e.g. the rapist was a stranger to the victim, he used extreme physical force, she resisted to the best of her ability) and the victim was deemed "worthy," not culpable (e.g. she had not been drinking or using drugs, she did not have a reputation for sexual "promiscuity," she was not dressed "provocatively," she was not out alone late at night), the filing of criminal charges was unlikely and a criminal conviction even less so. Similarly, acts of domestic violence, such as the aggravated assault of a wife by her husband, were also crimes, but the legal system – and the general public, for that matter – were steadfastly reluctant to invade the privacy of the family, thereby allowing husbands to "punish" their wives with impunity. Marxist, radical, and socialist feminists persistently (and loudly) challenged these social norms and legal practices and, as Goodmark (ibid.) observes, their "initiatives dovetailed with the growing societal desire to get 'tough on crime' and attracted backers interested in channeling resources into police and prosecution" (see also Richie, 2012).

It may be argued that these feminist efforts to change public policies, legal practices, and social norms have been more successful with regard to intimate partner violence than sexual assault (compare, for instance, Caringella, 2008 with Goodmark, 2012). But it is also the case that many of these successes have given rise to tensions and debates among various groups of feminists.[9] Objections, for example, have been raised to the portrayal of women as subordinated and in need of being "rescued," which denies women's agency and overlooks the many ways that women actively (and justifiably) resist domination and subordination, including violence and abuse.[10] Feminist critics have also voiced concerns about what they see as the *essentializing* of women's experiences in these perspectives. That is, the emphasis on women's domination by and subordination to men depicts a female experience that is unitary or universal, privileging "the experiences of white, middle-class, heterosexual women over those of others. Instead . . . women stand at the intersection of various identities that construct them: race, sexual orientation, socioeconomic class, disability, and other defining characteristics" (Goodmark, 2012: 5).[11] Thus, some low-income women may not want their abusive partners arrested or jailed because it may result in the men losing their jobs, which in turn will negatively affect their well-being and that of their children. These women may prefer an alternative intervention that gets the abuse to stop, but that preserves the intimate relationship and doesn't involve the criminal legal system in their lives. Women of color, in particular, have expressed reluctance to call on the legal system for help, since they have often witnessed or directly experienced it as more oppressive than beneficial (see Richie, 2012, but also Wood, 2012). Goodmark (2012: 25) captures this sentiment well when she quotes from Melanie Shepard and Ellen Pence's (1999) work: "I think white women talked more as if the courts belonged to us [all women] and therefore should work for us, where [women of color] always saw it as belonging to someone else and talked more about how to keep it from harming us."

Without doubt, the theorizing, empirical research, and unrelenting social and political activism of Marxist, radical, and socialist feminist criminologists, often in support of or in partnership with survivors of violence and victim advocates, has influenced law and policy, the workings of the criminal justice system, and public opinion about violence against women in numerous positive ways. Opinion surveys show increased public awareness of "domestic violence" and violence against women as serious social problems that warrant a strong response from the criminal justice system, although there is evidence that many people continue to hold victim-blaming attitudes (Carlson and Worden, 2002; European Commission, 2010). Courses on violence against women are offered on numerous college and university campuses throughout the world, with some institutions offering special certification programs (see, for instance, http://wiki.preventconnect.org). School- and campus-based prevention and intervention programs are widespread (see, for instance, Potter and Banyard, 2011). There are university-based research centers focused on violence against women (Jordan, 2011) and countless local, regional, national, and international governmental and non-governmental organizations addressing multiple dimensions of the problem. Boba and Lilley (2009) report that passage of the Violence Against Women Act (VAWA) has directly contributed to reductions in the rates of rape and assault in the United States.

Other studies show that law enforcement responses to intimate partner violence incidents have improved markedly over the past two decades, in the U.S. (Gover *et al.*, 2011) and in other countries as well (Gracia *et al.*, 2008). Nonetheless, significant problems remain, particularly in police and prosecutors' handling of sexual assault cases (Kaukinen and DeMaris, 2009; Kelly, 2010; Lonsway and Archambault, 2012; Spohn and Tellis, 2012). In fact, evidence indicates that the previously quoted concern about the harmful impact of the criminal justice system on women and men of color is well founded (see, for instance, Dylan *et al.*, 2008; Nash, 2005; Potter, 2008; Richie, 2012). In the next chapter, then, we examine feminist theorizing on the *intersections* of gender, social class, and race, as well as other social locating factors.

4

IDENTITIES AND INTERSECTIONALITIES

STRUCTURED ACTION THEORY, LEFT REALISM, POSTMODERN FEMINISM, AND BLACK/MULTIRACIAL FEMINIST CRIMINOLOGY

Let me begin with a confession: I struggled with the title for this chapter. For one thing, including all the theories to be discussed makes for an accurate, but not very eloquent title. It certainly does not roll easily off the tongue. More importantly, I do not want to give the impression that this is a "kitchen sink" chapter; that this is the chapter in which one throws in anything and everything that has not yet been covered but needs to be. Such would diminish the significance of each of the theories – an outcome that is opposite to what I intend and also somewhat ironic given that "othering" is a primary concern of these theories. It may also appear at first glance that, apart from the feminist tie, this is a theoretically disparate list. But as I will show, these theories are linked in several ways and together they have made a significant impact on criminology and criminal justice. To begin, then, let us examine the notion of gender as "situated accomplishment" and consider how it has been applied to the study of criminal offending.

MASCULINITIES, FEMININITIES, AND CRIME

As we noted in Chapter 1, *sex* and *gender* are terms typically used interchangeably in everyday conversation, but sociologists distinguish *sex*, a biological category, from *gender*, a socially constructed category. Nevertheless, even in sociological analyses, both sex and gender were – and, unfortunately, often still are – presented as binaries: categories with two mutually exclusive components. An individual is *either* male *or* female (sex), masculine *or* feminine (gender), and their masculinity or femininity derives "naturally" from their biological sex. A radical departure from this framework was introduced in 1987 by Candace West and Don Zimmerman in what has since become "the most cited article ever published in *Gender & Society*," one of the most prestigious academic journals in the fields of sociology and women's studies (Jurik and Siemsen, 2009: 72). Not only did West and Zimmerman attempt to break with the gender binary, they also replaced the traditional conceptualization of gender as a role or attribute of individuals with a more fluid, dynamic conceptualization of gender as accomplishment. Less than ten years later, West and Fenstermaker (1995) expanded the "doing gender approach" to other social categories, such as race and class, in an examination of the interactional aspects of "doing difference."[1] The doing gender/difference approach is also often referred to as *social construction feminism* because it sees gender as being socially created through people's actions and interactions with one another on a daily basis. The build-up of these interactions in the course of everyday life produces not only gendered self-identities, but also gendered social structures that, as Lorber (2009: 245) put it, "congeal" inequality.

To understand this perspective better, let us begin with the observation that social behavior is governed by norms, including gender norms (i.e. rules about masculinity and femininity), and these norms vary by social context or situation, although one consistent outcome is differentiation. In learning these norms, we learn how to "correctly" categorize people – and ourselves (e.g. male *or* female). As we interact, we constantly engage in this categorization, and we also know that others are categorizing us, so we make choices about how we look and act in a given situation based on how we think others might interpret our appearance and behavior. Social constructionists call this process *accountability*. Thus, people "do gender" by appearing and acting in ways that will lead others to identify them in a given situation as "male" or "female." Likewise, one may "do race" to be identified "white" or "Latino" or another race; one may "do sexual orientation" to be identified "gay" or "straight"; and so on. But this is not a process of constructing separate but equal categories, because these categories and the normative traits and behaviors attached to them are also ascribed differential value; some categories are valued more highly than others, and this inequality is reflected and reproduced in social relations and social structures in which people interact everyday – in, for example, families, schools, workplaces. As individuals continuously do gender (or race, or class), then, their "performance" is both constrained by and reproduces these unequal social relations and structures (West and Fenstermaker, 1995).

Before discussing how feminist criminologists have applied social constructionism in their theorizing and research, let us take a closer look at some of the central elements of this perspective. Notice first the importance of agency in social constructionism. From this perspective, individuals do not passively internalize pre-scripted gender roles that subsequently determine their attitudes and behavior; rather, gender is something people must do, or accomplish, in their everyday interactions with others (Connell, 1995). Moreover, how people do gender and what they accomplish varies situationally and is influenced by structural conditions. This means, then, that gender is not static or fixed. Social constructionism allows for multiple varieties of gender, for masculinit*ies* and femininit*ies*, that an individual will likely change – and may change dramatically, in fact – as their circumstances change (Miller, 2002). It also allows for the possibility that in some situations individuals may "improvise" their performance of gender, or innovate new ways of doing gender (Messerschmidt, 1997).

But while this element of agency is critical, keep in mind, too, that social constructionists recognize the importance of how structural constraints – for example, in the form of power differences within and across groups – impinge on how gender and other differences can be accomplished. One may be more powerful than others in one context (e.g. a husband exercising power over his wife and children at home), but less powerful than others in a different context (e.g. the same man being subject to the power of his boss at work). "Consequently," as Messerschmidt (1997: 7) argues, "rather than viewing gender, race, and class as discreet 'things' that somehow relate to each other, it is important to visualize them as mutually constituting one another . . ." Furthermore, as Lorber (2009: 245) points out:

> While the social construction perspective allows for changes in gendered practices, change does not come easily, because many of the foundational assumptions of the gendered social order and its ubiquitous processes are legitimated by religion, taught by education, upheld by the mass media, and enforced by systems of social control.

It is James Messerschmidt who has been credited with pioneering the application of social constructionism to criminological theorizing and research through the development of his *structured action theory*. Although Messerschmidt has studied young women's involvement in crime, particularly in the context of street gangs (see Messerschmidt, 1995, 1997, 2002), much of his work focuses on understanding the relationship between masculinities and crime for as he correctly notes, for most criminologists the study of gender and crime means the study of women and crime. But men and boys are gendered too, and although historically they have been viewed as the "normal subjects" of criminological research, "the gendered content of their legitimate and illegitimate behavior has been virtually ignored" (Messerschmidt, 1993: 1; see also Messerschmidt, 1997, 2000).

In examining masculinities in relation to crime, Messerschmidt (1993, 1997) argues that crime is a resource used by men and boys to do gender – more specifically, to accomplish masculinity in a particular setting. Through secondary analyses of others' research as well as his own in-depth interviews with young men, Messerschmidt (2000, 2002) has studied how boys and men ascribe meaning to their behavior and make conscious choices, albeit in the context of structural constraints, about how to behave in a particular situation. He reports, for example, that boys and men living in disadvantaged urban neighborhoods use street crime, such as robbery, not only as a way of getting money or other valuable items, but also as a means for constructing a particular type of masculinity that he calls "hardman" (Messerschmidt, 1993). In another example – an analysis of the 1986 space shuttle *Challenger* disaster – Messerschmidt (1997) explores the construction of corporate masculinities by the white, middle-class managers and engineers involved in the launch decision that resulted in the deaths of all seven *Challenger* astronauts.

Importantly, Messerschmidt (1995, 1997) also discusses how crime may be a resource for some young women to construct particular femininities. He maintains, for instance, that girls in street gangs engage in behaviors, such as fighting and other forms of violence, that some observers might interpret as their attempts to act like boys, but to the girls themselves the behavior has a different meaning. These girls describe themselves as "feminine," but as acting "bad" (see also Jones, 2009). Messerschmidt (1995: 183) labels this femininity "bad-girl femininity," stating that the girls "are doing femininity in terms of activities appropriate to their sex category and in a specific social situation [i.e. the urban street gang]." Elsewhere, Messerschmidt (2002) describes third-wave feminism,[2] including the hip hop and Riot Grrrl subcultures, as constructing a "tough-girl femininity." Messerschmidt (ibid.: 465) makes the significant point that when women and girls are violent they are not just acting like or mimicking men and boys, but rather are "engaging in violence authentically as [women and] girls and as a legitimate aspect of their femininity." Their accomplishment of gender, though, like that of men and boys, is simultaneously shaped by various structural inequalities, such as sexism, racism, social class inequality, and heterosexism.

Structured action theory, as we have noted, advances our understanding of gender and crime in several ways. One important contribution is that it broadens the criminological lens beyond women's victimization. Recall that the feminist theories we discussed in Chapter 3 have been critiqued for overemphasizing women's victimization, subverting their agency and, perhaps inadvertently but nonetheless effectively, reinforcing stereotypes of female passivity and weakness. It follows from such stereotyping that the woman or girl who is aggressive or who "fights back" is anomalous, or worse, pathological, whereas the structured action theorist sees her as doing what everyone must do: accomplishing gender. What is more, in addition to drawing attention to the gendered nature of male criminal offending, structured action theorists do not depict male or female offenders as simply acting out a predetermined "gender role," but rather as actively constructing gender (and race, class and other differences) within the parameters of structural constraints through criminal offending. As Miller (2002: 434) points out, structured action theory "provides a means of bridging the agency/structure divide . . . but does so in a way thoroughly grounded in the contexts of structural inequalities such as those of gender, sexuality, race, class, and age." Criminologists who have conducted research informed by structured action theory have found that crime is not only a means for accomplishing gender in certain contexts, but also that efforts to do gender affect who is victimized. For instance, in their studies of the characteristics of hate crime (e.g. the group nature of the offending, perpetrators' language, their use of alcohol) as well as the characteristics of hate crime perpetrators and victims, Bufkin (1999) and Perry (2001) argue that hate crime is a resource used by some groups of young men to accomplish a particular type of masculinity, specifically, *hegemonic masculinity*: white, Christian, able-bodied, and heterosexual.[3]

Structured action theory, however, has been criticized on a number of grounds.[4] Some critics argue, for example, that the way structured action theory is often applied in criminological analyses is tautological. A tautology is circular reasoning. The concern here is with what critics characterize as structured action theorists' rather myopic view that "whatever groups of boys and girls, or men and women, do is a kind of gender" (Risman, 2009: 81). And as Miller (2002) notes, the tautology problem is related to a second criticism of structured action theory: the tendency to reinforce, rather than challenge, *gender dualism* or what we referred to earlier as the gender binary. For instance, when young straight men engage in gay bashing it is interpreted by structured action theorists as an effort to construct a specific masculine identity, and when young women in a street gang fight with rival gang members, it is interpreted as an effort to construct a specific feminine identity. But to paraphrase Risman (2009), why label behaviors adopted by groups of males or females as alternative masculinities or femininities just because the group itself is made up of biological males and females?[5] For one thing, constructing gender in some situations may not be a primary motivation. Second, as Miller's (2001) research shows, some girls and women strongly identify with boys and men and describe their behavior as masculine, not feminine; that is, they see themselves as "one of the guys." So despite the theoretical conception of multiple masculinities and femininities, these critics maintain that structured action theory often falls short in applying this notion to real-life males and females because of its "selective attention" to gender difference, thereby overlooking instances of "gender crossing," contradictory or contingent gender constructions, gender resistance, and efforts to "undo gender" (Butler, 1990; Jones, 2009; Miller, 2002, Risman, 2009). This concern is extended to studies of differences, such as race and social class, which intersect with gender. Such research shows tremendous variation both across *and within* social groups. For example, there is evidence that some African American gang girls take pride in masculine identities (Miller, 2001), while others embrace feminine identities (Messerschmidt, 2002), and still others are "aggressive for the streets, pretty for the pictures" as part of a strategy to stay safe and survive the very dangerous neighborhoods in which they live their everyday lives (Jones, 2009: 89; see also Miller, 2002, 2008).

It is interesting to note that this latter point actually supports structured action theory in terms of documenting a multitude of masculinities and femininities as well as the agency that social actors exercise in constructing these multiple identities – sometimes highly constrained in their efforts and at other times pushing back hard enough at these constraints to create alternatives and bring about change. But this diversity and both potential and realized social change are precisely what critics do not want structured action theorists to lose sight of. Certainly, it is not easy to think outside the gender binary/dualism box, but it is necessary if we are to understand and appreciate the rich complexity and diversity of people's lived experiences, which for some include criminal offending.

TAKING THE GENDERED NATURE OF CRIME SERIOUSLY: LEFT REALISM

In Chapter 3, we mentioned the emergence of a "new criminology" in the late 1960s and 1970s that was critical of mainstream criminologists for focusing on crimes committed by the powerless (e.g. street crime committed by young men of color in impoverished urban neighborhoods) and ignoring the crimes of the powerful (e.g. white-collar and corporate crime committed by wealthy, white businessmen; human rights violations committed by police or military personnel acting on behalf of governments). In the mid-1980s, though, another form of critical criminology was developed that, while not unconcerned with crimes of the powerful, nevertheless called for more criminological attention to street crime as well as the harsh social control techniques being adopted to address it (e.g. stop and frisk practices, saturation policing, three-strikes-and-you're-out sentencing laws).[6] This perspective, which originated in Great Britain, is known as *left realism*; left realists urged fellow critical criminologists to take crime in the streets, and its effects, seriously (Carlen, 1995).

Left realists acknowledge that many people are seriously harmed by white-collar, corporate, and governmental crime, but at the same time, they argue that many radical and Marxist criminologists have neglected the fact that "ordinary people," especially people who live in impoverished and working-class, high-crime neighborhoods, must cope daily with the severe negative consequences of predatory street crime and thus, rightly, fear it (Currie, 1992; Lea and Young, 1984). Moreover, de-emphasizing the significance of this type of crime relinquishes responsibility for responding to "the crime problem" to right-wing conservatives whose solution is to "crack down on crime," resulting in more people enmeshed in an increasingly draconian criminal justice system (DeKeseredy, 2011b; DeKeseredy and Schwartz, 2010). Such responses, however, may just compound crime's painful effects, since both perpetrators and victims typically live in the same communities and, not infrequently, in the same households.

In developing their theory, left realists originally drew heavily on Marxism as well as on mainstream strain and subcultural theories of crime. For instance, British left realists Lea and Young (1984) maintained that when people who are poor perceive their situation as unfair, they grow discontented and, if they have no legitimate way to address the inequity they are experiencing, they become increasingly frustrated. When unhappy, frustrated people are segregated together in whole communities of disadvantage, they form subcultures that encourage and legitimate criminal behavior.

Left realism has been criticized by criminologists on the political left (e.g. Carlen, 1995; Henry, 1999; Smart, 1990) as well as mainstream criminologists (e.g. Gibbons, 1994). But some critical criminologists see value in the left realist perspective, particularly in accounting for the crimes committed "behind closed doors by patriarchal, abusive men" (DeKeseredy, 2011b: 38). DeKeseredy and Schwartz (2010) distinguish their brand of left realism from other iterations of the theory by foregrounding gender, noting that even recent revisions of left realism have been gender-blind, and by examining how gender intersects with race and social class to shape behavior, including criminal behavior.

DeKeseredy and Schwartz (2010) point out that laissez-faire economic policies in recent years have cost many men their jobs, as corporations move production overseas to countries where labor costs are lower and regulations are weak or nonexistent. Young, working-class men have been especially hard hit by deindustrialization and the restructuring of the economy in countries such as the U.S., Canada, and Great Britain. If they can find work, it is increasingly in low-paying and menial jobs. Yet, these men are steeped in their culture's gendered norms of hegemonic masculinity, including being self-reliant; taking responsibility as the family "breadwinner"; maintaining the "upper hand" over "their" women and children; being unemotional, tough, and aggressive; and steadfastly disdaining even the slightest appearance of femininity, so as not to be ridiculed as "gay" by male peers. If legitimate means (e.g. gainful employment) to live up to the principles of hegemonic masculinity are blocked, then other means, such as violence, may be used to accomplish this type of masculinity. According to DeKeseredy and Schwartz (ibid.: 163):

> Men at the bottom of the socioeconomic ladder flocking together with members of all-male sexist subcultures is not surprising, since they are more likely than their more affluent

> counterparts to adhere to an ideology of familial patriarchy . . . Arguably, such subcultures are likely to flourish in the near future because areas with high levels of poverty and unemployment are fertile breeding grounds for male-to-male and male-to-female violence . . .

In addition to theorizing how particular social constructions of masculinity combine with social class constraints to encourage criminal offending, DeKeseredy and Schwartz (2010) also examine the role of institutionalized racism, which exacerbates the impact of many social problems, including unemployment and under-employment, for men of color. Young black, Asian, Latino, and other minority men experience heightened negative effects of social and economic disadvantage, which block their ability to attain the masculine status they value. It is not surprising, then, that many of these young men support and reinforce one another's views regarding "respect," the use of drugs and alcohol, and the objectification and control of women, and engage in crime as a type of "compensatory masculinity" or as a means of "repairing 'damaged masculinity'" (ibid.: 164).

DeKeseredy and Schwartz's left realism may be considered a form of feminist left realism. Others (e.g. Carlen, 1995) have also identified compatibilities between left realism and feminism. Yet, one of the difficulties with left realism, even of the feminist variety, is that it does not pay much attention to female offending. Left realism focuses on how and why socially and economically marginalized men victimize one another as well as their female intimate partners and women in their communities. But these women share this disadvantaged status. Can women's lower rates of offending be explained simply in terms of their adherence to gendered norms of "emphasized femininity" (Messerschmidt, 1997)? That raises the tautology problem that we noted earlier with regard to structured action theory. More empirical research is needed to test the applicability of feminist left realism to women's offending as well as women's resistance to men's violence. At the same time, while DeKeseredy and Schwartz (2010: 164) acknowledge that there are "diverse subcultural ways of doing masculinity" such that there are many marginalized men who are nonviolent and who treat women with dignity just as there are many affluent men who abuse women, neither of these two groups is carefully studied by feminist left realists.[7] DeKeseredy and Schwartz (ibid.: 163) point out, for example, that "there is a large empirical and theoretical literature on the strong correlation between patriarchal male peer support and various types of woman abuse in university/college dating, which involves, for the most part, middle- and upper-class young adults . . ." Is this literature grounded in feminist left realism, or is feminist left realism limited to explaining only the criminal offending of socially and economically disadvantaged men? It is likely that the middle- and upper-class young *female* adults on university campuses, who are disproportionately affected by the offending of their male peers, would argue that this crime, too, should be "taken seriously." This is not to indict DeKeseredy and Schwartz, both of whom are recognized internationally as pro-feminist men and pioneering violence-against-women scholars, but rather to point out that the broader applicability of feminist left realism remains to date largely untested.

POSTMODERN FEMINIST CRIMINOLOGY

Most of us, throughout our lives, are exhorted to "tell the truth." We accept unquestioningly that there is an objective truth to be told. Similarly, most scientists, including criminologists and other social scientists, undertake empirical research in the pursuit of truth. Indeed, one of the foundational principles of science is that truth is knowable. But there is a group of criminologists who reject this claim. They are *postmodern* criminologists. Truth to postmodernists is a social construction, or, as postmodern feminist Nancy Wonders (1999: 116) explains:

> what passes for objectivity and the "truth" is really just one possible story about reality. . . . Thus, truth is always *contingent* on historical understandings, particular circumstances, and individual judgments; truth, therefore, is always temporary and partial – it can always change. Truth is also always political, privileging some perspective over others.

Postmodern theory has its origins in Europe, primarily France and Germany, where in the 1970s and 1980s, philosophers, literary theorists, and sociologists such as Jacques Derrida, Jean-Francois Lyotard, and Jean Baudrillard developed it as a sweeping critique of science, philosophy, and modernity. The theory quickly gained a sizeable following among academics in a variety of disciplines, including criminology, in Great Britain, Australia, and the United States during the 1980s and 1990s. Within criminology, various strains of postmodern theory have emerged, including postmodern feminist theory, and these, like left realism, have been critiqued by both the right and the left. One common criticism is that postmodernists' use of "jargonistic and insider language" does more to obfuscate than to elucidate their theoretical tenets; in fact, postmodernist prose has not infrequently been described as convoluted, incomprehensible, and vacuous (see, for example, Akers and Sellers, 2008; Naffine, 1995). Others maintain that postmodern criminologists offer little in the way of useful suggestions for public policy changes or an agenda of social activism, adopting instead a politically neutral stance or, worse, appearing reactionary at times (see, for instance, Friedrichs, 2009). Postmodern criminologists themselves often strongly criticize the ideas of fellow postmodernists (see, for example, Howe, 2000). Consequently, I undertake this attempt to offer a simplified, general overview of postmodern feminist criminology fully aware that I am unlikely to please or satisfy many criminologists, especially postmodern criminologists of any stripe.[8]

As noted at the outset of this section, postmodernists conceptualize "truth" as *contingent* or relative, not absolute. What is accepted as truth changes over time, and across places, and from one individual to the next. In the late 1800s, for example, it was widely accepted as a scientifically established truth that criminals were evolutionary throwbacks who could easily be identified by certain anatomical characteristics or "stigmata" such as big ears, a sloping forehead, and facial asymmetry, but today we understand this perspective to be fiction. Postmodernists, then, examine how realities are constructed through social interaction. However, unlike the social constructionists whose work we discussed earlier in the chapter, postmodernists do not emphasize social structure; they focus instead on culture, especially language, or *texts*. A text may be what we conventionally mean by the word – i.e. books, newspapers, diaries, or other written artifacts – but postmodernists also expand the term to include anything that people "read" or give meaning to. Every text has a *discourse*, that is, "what it says, does not say, and hints at (sometimes called a *subtext*)" (Lorber, 2009: 268). Also included in a text's discourse are the historical and social contexts and material conditions under which it is produced, as well as its intended audience (even though people in the actual audience may end up "reading" it differently from what the creators intended) (Lorber, 2009).

A central task for the postmodernist is to *deconstruct* or *decode* a text to expose or "unpack" its covert messages; that is, all the taken-for-granted assumptions, arbitrary distinctions, group interests, and values that undergird any "truth claim." In Humphries' (1999) analysis of "crack mothers," for instance, she shows how media reports, frequently drawing on medical and social science research that has since been widely criticized, constructed images "linking race, addiction, poverty, sexuality, and motherhood [and] turned the country's least powerful group, poor women of color, into a potent symbol of all that was wrong with America" (Humphries, 2013: 37). And despite the childhood chant that "words can never hurt me," such cultural representations often have very real and harmful consequences in people's lives because they promote particular courses of action. In this case, instead of offering treatment to substance-abusing women, some women were prosecuted in high-profile trials on charges of child abuse or endangerment, or for "delivering drugs to a minor;" many lost custody of their children.

In this example we also see another major concern of postmodernists: That some individuals and groups are able to get their values and beliefs represented as "truth," while others "do not participate in the construction of 'truth' because they have been systematically excluded from access to the tools of science, the power of the state, and the writing of history" (Wonders, 1999: 116). This exclusion has been based on difference, which is typically constructed as a dichotomy – e.g. male or female, heterosexual or homosexual, white or non-white – with one category ascribed greater value and, therefore, greater privilege, than the other. Although the differences that are used to divide members of these respective categories are represented as "natural" or biologically based, which gives the false impression that they are stable and largely immutable, postmodern analyses demonstrate how these categories in fact vary and change over time and across place or location. The U.S. Census provides a vivid example. The Census Bureau asks people to self-identify their race, but gives them predetermined categories from which to choose their racial identification; these categories, however, have changed in some way almost every decade since the 1800s. In 1890, for instance, there were eight racial categories on the census form, four of which were used to distinguish black people: you were "black" if you had three-quarters or more black ancestry, "mulatto" if you had three-eighths to five-eighths black ancestry, "quadroon" if you had one-quarter black ancestry, and "octoroon" if you had one-eighth or "any trace" of black ancestry. By 1900, there were five categories because "mulatto," "quadroon," and "octoroon" had been eliminated. Just 30 years later, in 1930, though, there were ten racial categories on the census form: white, negro, Indian (American Indian), Chinese, Japanese, Korean, Filipino, Hindu, Mexican, and "other." The 1930 census was the first and only time "Mexican" was identified as a distinct race. By 1950, Korean and Hindu (which is a religion) were deleted from the census form. Obviously, these dramatic changes on the census do not reflect actual changes in "races"; rather, they are the results of the fluctuating social, economic, and political concerns of those with the power to make "truth claims" about "race": the dominant white population during each historical period (Lee, 1993; see also Muhammad, 2010). "Thus, race is produced and reproduced all the time; indeed, we are continually changing the meaning of race" (Wonders, 1999: 117).

But by revealing the non-neutral, value-laden, often unjust character of various texts, postmodernists' deconstructions present the possibility of alternatives: If truth is provisional, individuals may reject, subvert, or appropriate specific depictions of "reality" and essentially reconstruct "reality" from their own standpoints and experiences. And herein lies the potential for social change from a postmodern perspective. In fact, it has been argued that while postmodern criminology on its own appears politically neutral or, worse, "intellectually and politically bankrupt" (Howe, 2000: 221), postmodern criminology joined with feminist criminology offers strategies for constructing "justice." For instance,

Wonders (1999: 122), drawing on Elam's (1994) concept of "ethical activism" argues that, "We have a responsibility – and obligation to ourselves and others – to understand our daily role in defining and creating reality and justice, and to do our best to make judgments that make the world a good place to be for all of us." Similarly, Grant (1993) urges the use of deconstruction to actively resist the negative, harmful, and hierarchical group identities that have been constructed by the powerful for the oppressed. Nevertheless, postmodern feminists continually caution against falling into the trap of advocating universal solutions to any social problem and warn criminologists not to assume we know what is "best" for oppressed groups. Justice, like all other "texts," is contingent: it changes over time, across location, and among individuals and groups. Thus, "local people everywhere need to develop their own definitions of their experiences and to work out their own methods of resistance to oppression" (DeKeseredy and Schwartz, 1996: 274).

There are, not surprisingly, many criminologists, including feminist criminologists, who find these postmodern and postmodern feminist strategies unsatisfying or insufficient. Some critics see such approaches as too individualistic, as little more than exhortations to "play nice" and make "good life choices," which do little to address or attack the inequalities embedded in major social institutions, such as the legal system (see, for example, Lorber, 2009). Others are critical of the strict relativism of postmodern feminism – for instance, the position that all knowledge is subjective, that "reality" is unknowable. Flavin and Artz (2013: 23), who have conducted extensive research on violence against women in post-apartheid South Africa, articulate this concern well:

> It is easy to argue that there is no essential experience with violence (and structural discrimination) for women in South Africa. However, it could also be argued that it is the very historical experience, and the horrific social impact of this experience, that may somehow be the binding agent of South African women. To no small extent, there are shared histories (apartheid rule), a common current reality (high risk of indiscriminate violence, including sexual violence) and a

> struggle (such as being free from violence, securing freedom of movement and a responsive criminal justice system) affecting all women. Are these issues not sufficiently common to South African women as women? Do they need to be entirely exposed and divided into individual segments so that each experience or struggle is so finely deconstructed and dissected that feminist advocacy is fractured? What is feminist theory if the core of it is not about women; some common thread of experience that differentiates us from men or masculinist law or justice? What makes it feminist? In this context, the weighty cautions and strict rationing of legitimate voices by feminism is counterintuitive.

While the uncompromising relativism of postmodern feminist theory has been viewed by some criminologists as actually undermining feminism, other feminist criminologists continue to challenge the discipline's tendency to ignore the significant impacts of multiple, simultaneous inequalities. An analysis of what has been called the "matrix of domination and resistance" (Collins, 2000) is the primary focus of black and multiracial feminist criminologists whose work we examine next.

INTERSECTIONALITY: BLACK AND MULTIRACIAL FEMINIST CRIMINOLOGY

Black feminist sociologist, Patricia Hill Collins (2012), in a recent reflection on her experiences teaching a course on "Contemporary Black Women" in a Black Studies department during the 1980s while she was writing her book, *Black Feminist Thought* (1990), reports that she avoided using the term "feminism" in class because her students strongly rejected it. "In their minds, feminism was for white women, not them" (Collins, 2012: 19). Indeed, Collins' students' complaints about feminism were widespread among women of color, particularly women of color in the academy, who, during the 1970s and 1980s, pointed to the fallacy of essentialist thinking in mainstream feminist scholarship and theorizing, which purported to speak on behalf of *all* women (Higgenbotham, 2012). Criminologist Amanda Burgess-Proctor (2006), citing Thompson (2002), points out, in fact, that second-wave feminism was often referred to by women of color and antiracist white women as "hegemonic feminism" because it regarded the experiences of white, middle-class, heterosexual women as the normative standard. Women academics of color, as "outsiders within the ivory tower" (Higgenbotham, 2012: 25), were well situated to see that one's standpoint or social locations shape one's construction of knowledge or "truth" and that knowledge production is never divorced from power relations (Baca Zinn, 2012; Collins, 2012; Yuval-Davis, 2012). This critique, and the alternative theorizing it generated, became the foundation on which black and multiracial feminist criminology was built.

Collins (1986, 1990) and others (e.g. Baca Zinn *et al.*, 1986; Baca Zinn and Thornton Dill, 1996; Crenshaw, 1994; Rice, 1990) argued that although hegemonic feminists acknowledge differences across groups of women, this acknowledgment rarely moves beyond a "tolerance" of pluralism, or as Baca Zinn and Thornton Dill (1996: 323) put it, "a long list of diversities which begin with gender, class, and race, and continue through a range of social structural as well as personal characteristics" (see also Laslett and Brenner, 2000). Overlooked, though, are differences of *power* among women that are attached to these "diversities." In addition, hegemonic feminism foregrounds gender inequality – specifically, dominance of men over women – while leaving unaddressed other subordinating statuses based on race, social class, sexual orientation, and other social locating factors that intersect with gender to produce different experiences of oppression and privilege. In other (and rather simplistic) words, women of color may experience sexism at the hands of men, including men of color, but they (and men of color) also experience racism in their interactions with white men *and* white women. Black and multiracial feminism, then, emphasizes both the *power relations* embedded in socially constructed differences and the *intersectionality* of these differences.

Black and multiracial feminism, therefore, is distinct from hegemonic and other feminisms in several significant ways. First, as we have already noted, black and multiracial feminists examine how various social locating factors – gender, race, ethnicity, social class, sexuality, age, national origin, physical ability – "*mutually construct one another* as unjust systems of power" (Collins, 2012: 19, emphasis added). Each of these social locations is structured hierarchically, with differential power and privilege attached to each rung of each hierarchy. But the hierarchies do not operate side by side; rather, they are overlapping hierarchies, forming what has been variously called the "matrix of domination" (Collins, 2000), "multiple marginality" (Richie, 1996), or "multiplicative identity" (Wing, 2003), because all women and men occupy rungs of all the hierarchies simultaneously (i.e. we are, at once, gendered, raced, classed, and so on, even though in any given situation one or two of these factors may have more salience than others). "[Y]ou cannot look at one of these social statuses alone, nor can you add them one after another. Their interaction is synergistic – together they construct social locations that are oppressive because they result in multiple systems of domination" (Lorber, 2009: 198).[9] These interlocking inequalities shape who we are as individuals and our interactions with one another within the groups to which we belong and across social groups, as well as our access to opportunities, rewards, privileges, and power. This means, then, that these interlocking hierarchies operate both at the institutional (macro) level and within the realm of everyday (micro) social interaction.

The omnipresence of these intersecting hierarchies or inequalities, however, does not mean that people are completely determined by them and lack agency. Nor does it mean that all members of the same group have the same experiences or that they "agree on the significance of [their] varying experiences" (Collins, 2000: 25). Thus, people's simultaneously held multiple identities will result in members of a specific group facing both common and divergent challenges, to which they may sometimes respond in unified, and at other times in diverse, ways. To paraphrase Potter (2006: 112), the experiences of women of color are collective, yet also individualized. This observation raises another fundamental principle of black and multiracial feminism: that all people are *both* privileged *and* oppressed; no one enjoys total privilege or suffers total oppression. Closely associated with this idea is the concept of *relationality*, which "assumes that groups of people are socially situated in relation to other groups of people based on their differences" (Burgess-Proctor, 2006: 37). Burgess-Proctor illustrates this point by noting that "some women benefit from the oppression of other women who occupy a lower social position, even when (or perhaps especially when) the former are not cognizant of the benefits that their privileged status provides" (p. 37). Baca Zinn and Thornton Dill (1996) underline the importance of this point by noting that while the intersectional framework was developed by black and multiracial feminists, it applies not only to women of color, but to all groups of women *and* men, because everyone experiences advantages and disadvantages resulting from intersecting inequalities.

Before turning to an assessment of the impact of black and multiracial feminism on feminist criminology, let us first discuss some of the concerns about this perspective that have been raised by feminist sociologists and criminologists. One issue has to do with the anti-essentialism of black and multiracial feminism and is similar to the objection voiced in regards to the relativism of postmodern feminism. Ngaire Naffine (2002), for instance, agrees that the perspectives and experiences of white, middle-class, heterosexual, and well-educated feminists long dominated feminist theorizing, scholarship, and activism, further marginalizing the voices of women from already marginalized groups. At the same time, however, she cautions against the counter-approach, which she sees as an overemphasis on what she calls "localized narratives": "The concerted effort to do justice to the world views of those differently situated, by declaring them the final authority on their own situation, contains the tacit proposition that their experience is somehow always beyond reach, always in some way incommensurable to one's own experience" (ibid.: 91; see also Rudy, 2000). Flavin and Artz (2013: 23) echo this concern, drawing again on their research in South Africa, where they note that despite the existence of 11 official languages and many more cultural groups, as well as tremendous variations in income and education, shared experiences among women nevertheless exist.

> If we assert that the lived experiences of women are all, always, so radically different from each other, then the future is grim indeed for feminist legal and criminological scholarship and policymaking. The end result is an analysis of women and their relationship to law and criminal justice that is so fragmented

> and oppositional that feminist jurisprudence and feminist reforms are simply too obscure and idiosyncratic to be tenable.

Some critics have also expressed the related concern that black and multiracial feminism produces "identity politics," which is also divisive and exclusionary because it assumes that only those who share the same marginal or oppressed identity or social location can truly understand it. Collins (1990), though, and others (e.g. Yuval-Davis, 2012) explicitly reject this position, with Harding (1993: 59) labeling it "ethnocentric." Yuval-Davis (2012: 51) emphasizes that advocates do not necessarily have to be members of the group for whom they are advocating, since "it is the message, not the messenger, that counts." She further cautions advocates who are members of the groups for whom they are advocating not to assume they can speak for everyone in their group. She points out that one of the problems with identity politics is that outspoken activists and "community leaders" often become identified as the "authentic voice" of their communities, and this may be harmful to other members, such as women, who may be marginalized *within* these communities. In her admonition she highlights the significance of intersectionality: "even as advocates, it is important that the activists should be reflective and conscious of the multiplexity of their specific positionings" (Yuval-Davis, ibid.; see also Rudy, 2000).

Finally, some critics have argued that the focus on intersecting inequalities may produce an "oppression olympics" (Hancock, 2011), in which various groups vie for recognition as "most oppressed," again producing divisiveness, rather than solidarity, across marginalized groups and undermining efforts toward progressive social change. While examples of this problem certainly exist, especially during periods when marginalized groups are forced by economic recession and budget cuts to compete with one another for limited funding and other resources, this criticism also stems from a misunderstanding (and perhaps, misuse) of black and multiracial feminism generally, and of intersectionality in particular. Collins (1997), for example, sees no value in constructing hierarchies of oppression. For one thing, she maintains, there is no single "worst" position. In addition, she believes that in order to arrive at an approximation of "truth" it is crucial to engage in dialogue with people holding various social positionings – not only those on the margins, but also those in the "hegemonic center."

Regardless of these criticisms, the impact of black and multiracial feminism, particularly the intersectionality framework, on feminist criminology cannot be overstated.[10] Baca Zinn (2012: 30) asserts that, "In the past three decades, intersectionality has become a sociological specialty in its own right, with unique concepts, methodologies, and a distinctive process through which knowledge is shaped. Today, the distinguishing features of intersectionality are part of the gender studies canon." Her observation characterizes feminist criminology equally as well. Let us consider, then, some examples of this influence.

INTERSECTIONALITY IN FEMINIST CRIMINOLOGICAL RESEARCH

Feminist criminologists began calling for greater attention to intersecting inequalities – in particular, the intersections of gender, race, and class – in criminological research in the late 1980s and 1990s (see, for example, Daly, 1993, 1997; Daly and Stephens, 1995; Hill and Crawford, 1990; Simpson, 1991; see also Britton, 2000). In the ensuing years, a large number of studies have examined how intersecting inequalities based on gender, race, class, age, and sexuality construct and constrain the life experiences of various groups of women and men, including their experiences as criminal offenders and as crime victims. Much of this work has focused on violent crime and has shown how, especially for young women of color growing up in severely disadvantaged neighborhoods, violent victimization is intimately tied to violent offending. For instance, Nikki Jones' (2010) ethnographic research with African American inner-city girls reveals the various strategies these young women use to deal with the very real threats to their survival posed by living in impoverished communities plagued by an active and violent drug trade and a hyper-masculine "code of the street." Although their male peers confront the same environmental conditions, Jones shows how both the threats of violence and the adolescents' responses to them are gendered, with girls' use of violence being in some ways similar to, but in other ways distinct from, boys' use of violence, and how use of violence varies even among girls who share these circumstances (see also Miller, 2008). Jones examines how the young women feel pressure to conform to the idealized notion of the "good, respectable girl," but how some also feel the need to construct a public image as a "tough girl" or a "fighter" as a way to protect themselves at school or in their neighborhood. Such a public persona, though, may result in harsh responses to their violent behavior by teachers, the police, and judges, increasing their risk of being expelled from school, arrested, and placed in a juvenile detention facility, a point that we return to shortly.

We see in Jones' research not only how gender, race, class, and age intersect to shape vulnerability to violence, but also potential victims' efforts to prevent or resist such violence. Recent research on intimate partner violence reinforces the importance of analyzing intersectionality in order to develop a fuller understanding of victimization, resistance, and offending. For example, Hillary Potter (2006, 2008) considers, among other factors, how interactions within the black community based on distinctive aspects of black culture explain African American women's experiences of and responses to intimate partner violence. Potter (2006: 116) reports, for instance, that:

> Black women remain in abusive relationships more so out of fear of being without companionship, being without a father or father figure for minor children, and being stigmatized as yet another single black mother than fear of further and more perilous battering incidents or of financial independence.

She sees these fears as direct outgrowths of African American women's unique experiences in U.S. society as well as within the African American community.[11] Moreover, she identifies the image or ideal of the "Strong Black Woman," which has developed out of African American women's need to confront various types of domination and discrimination in their everyday lives, as playing a critical role in influencing their responses to intimate partner violence. More specifically, as "Strong Black Women," African American women are more likely than other women to fight back against their abusive partners (Potter, 2008; see also Garfield, 2005; Gillum, 2002; Richie, 1996, 2012).[12]

It may be argued, however, that it is in research on criminal justice processing, particularly sentencing, that one can see the greatest influence of black and multiracial feminism. Consider, for instance, recent feminist criminological analyses of *sentencing disparity*, which occurs when offenders charged with the same or a similar crime are given different punishments. Looking at the data in Table 4.1, we see that racial and ethnic minorities, both male and female, are disproportionately represented among state and federal prison populations. While black men make up 13.2 percent of the U.S. male population, they are 38.8 percent of the U.S. male *prison* population. Similarly, Hispanic men are 16.5 percent of the U.S. male population, but 22.6 percent of the U.S. male prison population. The disparities are less dramatic for women, but are present nonetheless: Black women are 14.0 percent and Hispanic women 15.0 percent of the U.S. female population, respectively, but they are 25.4 percent and 17.9 percent of the U.S. female prison population, respectively (Guerino *et al.*, 2012). Women, though, regardless of race, make up a very small percentage of the prison population in the United States (less than 7 percent), although the number of women incarcerated in state and federal prisons has increased dramatically since 2000 and at a rate higher than that of men (ibid.). Are these differences

Table 4.1 Estimated number of sentenced prisoners under State and federal jurisdiction, by sex and race, 2010

Race	**Sex**	
	Male	**Female**
White	451,600	48,000
Black	561,400	26,600
Hispanic	327,200	18,700
Total	1,446,000	104,600

Source: Guerino *et al.*, (2012: 26).

across groups caused solely by legal factors (e.g. crime severity, previous record), or do extra-legal factors, such as the offenders' race and/or sex, influence sentencing decisions thereby producing sentencing disparities? Studies by feminist criminologists utilizing an intersectionalities framework have begun to answer such questions.

Traditionally, criminologists would approach the question of how extra-legal factors affect sentencing decisions by looking at a single variable at a time: sex *or* race. For example, data consistently show that, among adults, female defendants are significantly less likely than male defendants to be sentenced to prison, and even when women are sentenced to prison, their incarceration periods are shorter, on average, than those of men. These differences are found not only in the United States, but in the United Kingdom, Australia, and New Zealand, too (Spohn and Brennan, 2013). Spohn and Brennan (ibid.) review numerous studies of gender disparities in sentencing and report that even when accounting for crime seriousness, prior criminal record, and other legally relevant factors, women receive more lenient sentences than men, a finding that suggests judges and juries view female offenders differently – perhaps as less threatening, perhaps as less blameworthy – than male offenders. Thus, gender stereotypes may be influencing sentencing decisions, but, drawing attention to the question of intersectionality, Spohn and Brennan (ibid.: 218) point out that, "What is generally missing from the extant theoretical literature is a discussion of how racial/ethnic stereotypes may condition gender stereotypes." Given that hegemonic culture constructs "the criminal" as a young, black or Latino male and the media consistently reinforce this image, judges and juries may be influenced by intersecting racial and gender stereotypes that associate threat, dangerousness, and criminality with men of color, but not women of color. There are, of course, negative racialized and gendered stereotypes of women of color, too (see, for instance, Gillum, 2002; Landrine, 1985) and the media generally treat minority female offenders less sympathetically than white female offenders (Brennan and Vandenberg, 2009).[13] How might the intersecting inequalities of gender and race affect sentencing outcomes, then? Spohn and Brennan (2013) report that women receive more lenient sentences than men of the same race, such that women of color fare better than men of color in sentencing, thereby benefiting from their gender status. At the same time, however, white women are afforded preferential treatment relative to white men *and* men of color, whereas black and Hispanic men are punished more harshly than white women, women of color, *and* white men, indicating that they pay a "race penalty" when sentenced.[14]

The brevity of this book does not allow me to adequately cover all of the important contributions being made by feminist criminologists whose work is framed by black and multiracial feminism. I do hope, however, that the sampling I have offered gives readers an inkling of black and multiracial feminism's impact on feminist criminology, as well as a strong sense of how black and multiracial feminism pushes criminologists beyond the conceptualization of gender, race/ethnicity, and other social locators as mere "control variables" and allows us to more fully understand the complexity of people's lived experiences. More startling – and energizing – is the fact that black and multiracial feminism is still in its infancy as criminological theory, and those of us who apply it in our work recognize the need for much more research that explores the multiple and intricate ways that gender intersects with race and ethnicity, social class, age, sexuality, ability, and other status markers to shape differential outcomes for crime victims and offenders, for students, and for criminal justice professionals. We have truly only scratched the surface. In Chapter 5, we'll suggest critical spots on this surface that we think warrant deeper and more vigorous scratching.

5

FUTURE DIRECTIONS IN FEMINIST CRIMINOLOGY

It is that time in the book to take stock of feminist criminology – to reflect on where it has been and to speculate on where it may be headed. This is at once an enticing and an intimidating task or, as sociologist Barrie Thorne (2000: 1183) characterized it with respect to her assessment of the past and future of women's studies in general, a task "laced with ambivalent feelings of satisfaction and unease." After all, a major theme running throughout this book has been that feminists do not speak with one voice. In light of the diversity of feminisms, then, it is not surprising that feminists disagree on the extent to which feminism has impacted criminological theory and research, criminology courses and the campus environment, and the practice of law and criminal justice. Even more challenging is the search for consensus among feminists regarding what directions feminist criminology will – and *should* – take in the years to come.[1] Ever the optimist (or the fool), I offer in this final chapter a brief accounting of feminist criminology's contributions and limitations, and I raise several substantive topics that I hope feminist criminologists will explore more fully in the near future.

HERE TO STAY: WOMEN STUDENTS AND FACULTY

The extent to which feminism has truly transformed criminology is a topic that continues to be debated. But less disputed is the fact that there are numerous indicators of substantial and positive contributions. We begin by considering "the numbers."

As we discussed in Chapter 2, the number of female undergraduate and graduate students increased dramatically from the 1960s to the 1980s. In the United States, for example, women were the majority of undergraduate students (52.3 percent) by 1980, although they were still fewer than 50 percent of bachelor's and master's degree recipients (47.3 percent and 49.3 percent, respectively) and less than a third of doctorates (29.8 percent) (Renzetti *et al.*, 2012). Since 1980, women's representation among undergraduate and graduate students has continued to grow; by 2007, 57.2 percent of undergraduate students in the U.S. were women. Even more dramatic was their increased representation among degree recipients: 57.2 percent of bachelor's degrees, 60.6 percent of master's degrees, and 50.1 percent of doctorates were awarded to women in June 2006 (Renzetti *et al.*, 2012). The majority of these students, however, are white – about 75 percent of all degree recipients in 2007, both male and female. But students of color have substantially increased their representation among degree recipients in the U.S. since the late 1970s, more than doubling their percentages of bachelor's degrees and doctorates from 1977 to 2007, and women of color have made greater gains than men of color. For example, African American women received 4.4 percent of doctorates awarded in 2009, up from 1.7 percent in 1980, compared with African American men, who received 2.2 percent of doctorates awarded in 2009 and 2.1 percent in 1980. In fact, for every major U.S. racial and ethnic group, the percentage of doctorates awarded to women increased between 1980 and 2009, whereas for men the percentages were relatively stable, although for native American/Alaskan native men, the percentage decreased slightly during this period (ibid.).

Criminology and criminal justice, fields of study traditionally dominated by men, have also seen a steady influx of female students at all levels of study since the 1980s. In 1982, for example, only 39 percent of bachelor's degrees in "law enforcement, criminology, and corrections" awarded by U.S. colleges and universities were awarded to women; in 2007, 48.9 percent of bachelor's degrees in "criminal justice and law enforcement administration" were awarded to women (Renzetti *et al.*, 2012; U.S. Department of Education, 1986).[2] At the graduate level, women are now a majority of degree recipients in criminology and criminal justice: 50.9 percent of master's degree recipients in 2007, and 54.5 percent of doctorates the same year (Renzetti *et al.*, 2012; see also Frost and Clear, 2007). An even larger percentage of current graduate students in criminology and criminal justice are women: 57 percent of currently active master's students and 59 percent of doctoral students (Rice *et al.*, 2007). Interestingly, looking at Table 5.1 we see that women of color make up a sizable percentage of degree recipients in "homeland security, law enforcement, and fire fighting," and typically outnumber men of color at the bachelor's and master's degree levels.

As some observers point out, if these enrollment trends continue, women will constitute the majority of criminology and criminal justice faculty in the not-too-distant future (Frost and Clear, 2007; Rice *et al.*, 2007), and these faculties are likely to have more women of color than men of color.[3] Currently, however, only about 35 percent of full-time criminology and criminal justice faculty are women (Rice *et al.*, 2007), and as Potter *et al.* (2011) argue, both gender and race factors impinge on women's academic productivity and, therefore, their success in the academy. Researchers, for instance, have found female faculty members devote more time to teaching and to institutional service (e.g. departmental and university committees) than male faculty members do. These heavier obligations are especially pronounced for female faculty of color, because students not only from their own racial/ethnic group, but from any marginalized group may seek them out for advice and assistance, and university and department administrators seeking to diversify committee membership will appoint them to multiple committees (ibid., 2011). Moreover, female faculty of color usually give their time generously because "they feel students of color need their assistance or that specific committees need their voice and representation" (Thomas and Hollenshead, 2001: 173; see also Gilbert and Tatum, 1999).

But time spent teaching, advising students, and engaging in committee work is time not spent on conducting research and publishing, which are the activities by which faculty achievement

Table 5.1 Degrees awarded in homeland security, law enforcement, and firefighting, U.S. colleges and universities, by sex and race/ethnicity, 2009–10

Bachelor's degrees (Total = 43,667)		
	Sex	
Race	Males (Total = 22,265)	Females (Total = 21,402)
White	15,202	11,250
Black	3,085	5,635
Hispanic	2,828	3,560
Asian/Pacific Islander	811	575
American Indian/Alaskan Native	191	215
Non-resident (international student)	148	167
Master's degrees (Total = 6,714)		
	Sex	
Race	Males (Total = 3,140)	Females (Total = 3,574)
White	2,205	2,010
Black	489	1,008
Hispanic	255	357
Asian/Pacific Islander	89	110
American Indian/Alaskan Native	27	36
Non-resident (international student)	75	53
Doctoral degrees (Total = 106)		
	Sex	
Race	Males (Total = 57)	Females (Total = 49)
White	35	36
Black	3	4
Hispanic	2	0
Asian/Pacific Islander	4	1
American Indian/Alaskan Native	1	0
Non-resident (international student)	12	8

Source: U.S. Department of Education, National Center for Education Statistics, 2012. Retrieved from http://www.nces.ed.gov/programs/digest/d11/tables/dt11_301.asp, dt11_304.asp, dt11_307.asp.

is typically judged. Not surprisingly, then, researchers have found a gender gap in publication rates, although it has narrowed since the 1970s, and in criminology, criminal justice, and sociology, when factors such as type of institution at which faculty work and years as a faculty member are controlled, the gap narrows more or closes completely (Keith *et al.*, 2002; Snell *et al.*, 2009; Stack, 2002). Another relevant factor is having a mentor; male and female criminologists who have mentors, especially male mentors, have more publications than criminologists without mentors (McElrath, 1990). Importantly, some studies indicate that female faculty of color are more likely than men and white women to have a mentor, although additional research indicates that female faculty of color do not consistently receive support from white female colleagues, and they are more likely to have fewer resources available, such as research assistants and start-up money, to facilitate their research (Gilbert and Tatum, 1999; Thomas and Hollenshead, 2001; Turner, 2002).

Potter and her colleagues (2011: 95) report another interesting finding: "female criminology faculty members are *more likely* than their male counterparts to publish articles if they believe articles advance the discipline" (authors' emphasis). In this regard, an important question is: What is perceived as advancing the discipline? Traditionally, advancing the discipline has been understood by criminologists as publishing not only in peer-reviewed journals, but in what are considered *elite* peer-reviewed journals, and these have tended to favor sophisticated statistical analyses. Some criminologists, including feminist criminologists, have been critical of this approach. Potter *et al.* (ibid.), for example, quote Elliott Currie (2007), who advocates for a "public criminology" in which criminological research is disseminated to a broader audience than our academic peers, such as policymakers and the general public. Potter *et al.* (2011) point out that heavy reliance on "out of reach statistical models" often alienates students as well as criminal justice professionals and practitioners who are "at the frontlines to affect change" (p. 97). Potter and her colleagues note, however, that feminist criminologists are more amenable to qualitative research methods, which makes their work more accessible to a broader audience and, therefore, more likely to affect criminal justice policy and practice. As we learned in

Chapter 1, affecting progressive social change is among the core objectives of feminism, including feminist criminology.

We take up the issues of research and publication again later in this chapter, but for now we want to return to the question of the impact of feminist criminology in the classroom, particularly in light of the data on gender and racial/ethnic composition of the student body. To what extent are these students being exposed to a curriculum infused with feminist criminology?

As mentioned in Chapter 2, during the 1970s and 1980s many criminology and criminal justice programs began to add courses on "women's issues" to their curriculum. These, we said, were usually "Women-in" and "Women-and " courses, and in evaluating the influence of these courses on students' perceptions and beliefs, the concern arose that they were perhaps reinforcing rather than debunking most students' gender stereotypes in that the courses were taught almost exclusively by female faculty and enrolled mostly female students. They were viewed as "niche courses," marginalized and devalued, while the integration of feminist criminological theory and research into the "mainstream" curriculum was strongly resisted. There are indications, however, that some, albeit limited, progress has been made with regard to curriculum integration in the intervening years.

Certainly, feminist criminologists themselves incorporate feminist theory and research into the general or required criminology and criminal justice courses they teach, and many teach from an intersectionality framework in doing so.[4] There are numerous feminist criminology and criminal justice textbooks now available to instructors, but "general" criminology and criminal justice textbooks have also begun to include feminist criminology. Consider, for example, that when Daniel Curran and I published the first edition of the criminological theory textbook, *Theories of Crime*, in 1993, it was one of only a handful of such texts to include feminist criminological theory. Today, nearly all criminological theory textbooks include feminist theory, although many still devote less than two pages to a discussion of what we have shown in the present book to be a diverse and complex paradigm.[5]

Course offerings have also expanded and, as already noted, many move well beyond the "Women-in" and "Women-and" formula of the 1970s and 1980s to incorporate intersectionality while de-essentializing not only gender, but also race, ethnicity, class, and sexuality. For instance, in reviewing the course offerings of 321 criminal justice-related degree programs in the United States, Patten and Way (2011) found that 67 percent offer at least one "diversity" course (i.e. a course that focuses on gender, race, and/or class), and 14 percent of the programs require such a course for their majors. But as Patten and Way emphasize, while these figures are encouraging they still mean that about a third of criminal justice programs do *not* offer any diversity courses and the vast majority (86 percent) do not require their students to take these courses. Also significant is the fact that two-thirds of the programs offer only *one* diversity course, and of the 488 diversity courses they identified, most focused *either* on women/gender (n = 239) *or* race/ethnicity (n = 212); only 37 courses included gender *and* race.

It is worth noting that in its most recently promulgated certification requirements for undergraduate criminal justice programs, the Academy of Criminal Justice Sciences (ACJS) states that the curriculum should include a systematic examination of diversity issues by integrating such issues into courses in the program's curriculum or by offering required courses focused specifically on diversity issues in criminal justice (ACJS, 2012). Such requirements may help to increase course offerings that incorporate an intersectional analysis of gender, race and ethnicity, social class, sexuality, and other status markers that underlie and sustain social relations of both inequality and opportunity in the academy and the criminal justice system.

Flavin and Artz (2013) discuss another alarming trend that threatens feminist criminology in the academy: "men's and masculinities studies." Flavin and Artz state that opponents of men's and masculinities studies see it as a "backlash to feminism," while proponents characterize it as a "parallel conversation" to feminism (p. 21). They argue that, "Sometime in the 1990s . . . masculinities theory became the new sweetheart and theoretical equalizer in critical criminology . . . emerg[ing] partly out of a response to radical feminist theories about men and their complicity in maintaining the status quo of men within social and political life" (ibid.). Regardless of its origins, more concerning is how it is negatively impacting the inroads feminist criminology has made in the curriculum. Flavin and Artz, for example, report that feminist methods and theories modules in the curricula of three majors schools of criminology at universities in South Africa were dramatically changed to allow for the expansion of "men and masculinities." Thus, while feminist criminology has contributed to the revitalization of radical and critical criminology (see DeKeseredy and Dragiewicz, 2013; Smart, 1990; Young, 1988), Flavin and Artz (2013: 21) conclude:

> This shift to masculinities studies has been perceived as a method of mollifying mainstream criminology. In retrospect, a focus on masculinities was an almost inevitable reaction to radical, vigorous and largely legal feminist projects whose primary concern was to achieve women's substantive equality, develop progressive social policy and to improve criminal justice . . .

The importance of feminist criminology to the criminology and criminal justice curriculum, especially feminist criminology that draws on the intersectionality framework, cannot be overestimated. As Patten and Way (2011) point out, many students studying for degrees in criminal justice-related programs wish to pursue careers as criminal justice professionals and practitioners. Given the growing diversity of most industrialized societies, criminal justice professionals and practitioners increasingly need to know how to communicate and interact effectively with women and men from diverse backgrounds and cultures. Sexism, racism, ethnocentrism, homophobia, and other forms of prejudice and discrimination may result not only in simple misunderstandings or miscommunications, but also in serious errors that cause injury and death. Indeed, Carol Smart (1990: 84) maintains that at this juncture criminology needs feminism more than feminism needs criminology, and even though many criminologists, "especially of the traditional variety," will balk at such a statement, she suggests that "they had better look at who their students are . . ."

ALSO HERE TO STAY: WOMEN IN THE CRIMINAL JUSTICE PROFESSIONS

In Chapter 2, we learned that legal challenges and legislative reforms contributed to an increase in the number of women working as police officers, attorneys, judges, and corrections officers. And as we noted earlier in this chapter, the large number of women graduating from colleges and universities with degrees in criminal justice-related majors is certainly increasing their representation among criminal justice professionals and practitioners. Today, for example, there are about 18,000 state and local law enforcement agencies in the United States with about 593,00 full-time employees, including 461,000 sworn officers; 60 percent of these sworn personnel are local police officers. About 1 in 8 local police officers are women, compared with 1 in 13 in 1987; 1 in 4 is an officer of color, compared with 1 in 6 in 1987 (Bureau of Justice Statistics, 2012). In other countries, too, the number of women police officers has grown fairly steadily in the last two decades, although as DeJong (2013) points out, outside of Europe and the United States, female officers' roles and responsibilities are typically restricted to working with women and children or in "special" rather than "regular" police units. In some countries, such as Brazil and India, female-only police units have been created to respond exclusively to cases of violence against women, because of widespread complaints that male officers did not respond appropriately (or at all) to female victims of such crimes (Nelson, 1996).[6] Nevertheless, one of the disadvantages of these all-female, specialized units is that officers are often regarded as "social welfare workers" rather than "real" police officers, and women officers in these units end up with few, if any, opportunities to transfer to other units or to advance in the profession (DeJong, 2013; Hautzinger, 1997).

DeJong (2013), in reviewing research on gender and policing, points out that until relatively recently, criminologists who studied police officers not infrequently had all-male samples, and most of these men were also white. Much of the research since the 1980s has addressed the question of whether women and men police differently. Although a discussion of this research is well beyond the scope of this book, suffice it to say that the findings are equivocal at best. As DeJong (ibid.) concludes, numerous factors, including situational context and the characteristics and demeanor of suspected offenders as well as complainants, influence police officers' behavior. Such factors appear to have a greater impact than officers' sex, race, ethnicity, or sexual orientation.

Nevertheless, studies do reveal some important differences in officers' on-the-job experiences, particularly in terms of interacting with fellow officers and supervisors. One significant issue, for instance, is the *sexualization* of the workplace. Researchers report that sexual teasing, jokes, and innuendo are routine in police departments, and female officers experience a good deal of sexual harassment, but usually do not report it for fear of retaliation by other officers or worries about being forced to resign (Collins, 2006; Horne, 2006; Lee, 2009). Unlike male officers – or, more accurately, because of male officers' attitudes and behavior – female police officers continue to have to strike a balance between trying to prove they are "as good as" or "equal to" the men and adopting behavior that may be perceived as traditionally feminine in order to win male officers' approval (Rabe-Hemp, 2009).[7] It appears, then, that despite the influx of women into policing in recent years, law enforcement remains an occupation dominated by the norms of hegemonic masculinity.

We may arrive at a similar conclusion when considering the practice of law. As Table 5.2 shows, in 2009–10, women were 47.2 percent of graduates from U.S. law schools, which represents a substantial increase since the 1980s, although women's law school enrollments have dipped slightly over the past ten years.[8] The vast majority of law school graduates continues to be white, but we see in Table 5.2 that women of color, particularly African American and Asian American women, are more likely than men of color to attain a law degree. Nevertheless, significant gender and race differences continue to characterize the field. For example, Siemsen and Candela (2013) describe the "hierarchy of law," in which partners and associates in large corporate firms have the greatest prestige (and income), while corporate counsel, lawyers in small firms, and solo practitioners tend to have less; government, legal aid, and public interest attorneys are ranked lowest. "Lawyers who work in legal aid or criminal law are tainted by their frequent exposure to social problems. . . . Women attorneys outnumber men in the least prestigious and most socially contaminated legal positions" (ibid.: 267). Roughly the same percentage of female attorneys as male attorneys hold government positions (13.5 percent and 13.2 percent, respectively), but nearly twice as many female attorneys as male attorneys practice public interest law (7.8 percent and 4.2 percent, respectively) (Catalyst, 2012). One recent analysis of the legal profession reported that there "is a drastic difference between women and men at the highest levels in law firms" (ibid.: 2). Although women were 31.9 percent of practicing attorneys in the United States in 2011, they were only 19.5 percent of partners in law firms. And while this percentage was a significant increase over 1995 when they were only 13.4 percent of partners, the report states that if the current rate of change continues, "it will take more than a woman lawyer's lifetime to achieve equality" (ibid.: 2). The disparity is even greater for female attorneys of color, who are only 2 percent of partners in U.S. law firms (Catalyst, 2012).

There is evidence that blatant gender bias in law firms and courtrooms is less common today than in the past (see, for instance,

Table 5.2 Law degrees (LL.B or J.D.) conferred by U.S. degree granting institutions, by sex and race, 2009–10

Total = 44,345	**Sex***	
Race	**Male (%)**	**Female (%)**
All races	23,394 (52.8)	20,951 (47.2)
White	18,362 (41.4)	14,653 (33.0)
Black/African American	1,211 (2.7)	1,995 (4.5)
Hispanic	1,550 (3.5)	1,632 (3.7)
Asian American/Pacific Islander	1,701 (3.8)	2,053 (4.6)
American Indian/Alaskan Native	179 (0.4)	189 (0.4)
Non-resident (International student)	391 (0.9)	429 (1.0)

*Percentages do not add to 100 due to rounding

Source: U.S. Department of Education, National Center for Education Statistics. Retrieved from http://www.nces.ed.gov/programs/digest/d11/tables/dt11_309.asp.

Samborn, 2002), but recent studies also highlight how the intersection of sexism and racism continue to have deleterious effects on the work experiences of female attorneys of color.[9] These studies show, for instance, that female attorneys of color are more likely than white female attorneys and male attorneys regardless of race to experience racial and gender stereotyping, to feel excluded by colleagues at work, to feel it necessary to make adjustments to "fit in" at work, to sense that their supervisors were not committed to diversity in promotion, and to consider leaving the firm where they were employed (Catalyst, 2012; see also American Bar Association, 2006, 2008). Such findings have led some observers to maintain that "[s]tructural resistance to women's and minorities' presence in the legal profession appears to be growing rather than subsiding" (Siemsen and Candela, 2013: 268; see also Kenney, 2008).

Arguably, however, it is in the field of corrections that women have encountered the greatest resistance to their employment. As with other criminal justice occupations, the number of female correctional officers, particularly in men's prisons, has grown substantially since the 1980s in the U.S., Canada, the U.K., and Australia, although women are still a relatively small percentage of jail and prison officers (Griffin, 2013). For example, in the U.S. there are twice as many male than female employees in state and federal correctional facilities (Stephan, 2008). Griffin (2013) has aptly characterized the contemporary working environment in most correctional facilities as "hyper-masculine."

Like the research on gender and policing, much research on gender and correctional employment has traditionally tried to determine whether female and male officers do their jobs differently. And like the research on gender and policing, the findings of these studies are inconsistent; some researchers report significant differences in female and male correctional officers' supervisory styles and attitudes toward the work, whereas others identify few differences (see Griffin, 2013, for a review of this research). Again, however, the work experiences of female and male correctional officers appear to be strikingly different. Female officers – whether in the U.S., Great Britain, Canada, or Australia – "report experiencing harassment and bullying by male colleagues, a highly segregated workplace, and limitations regarding assigned duties" (Griffin, 2013: 288). But the prison environment is racialized as well as sexualized, such that officers of color, but especially female officers of color, experience greater resistance, harassment, and discrimination (Britton, 1997, 2003; Griffin *et al.*, 2005). For instance, both male and female African American correctional officers express lower job satisfaction than their white peers, but African American female officers report greater job-related stress than either white female officers or male officers regardless of race (Britton, 1997). Female officers of color are also less likely than white female officers or male officers regardless of race to perceive the prison organization as equitable and consistent in terms of its treatment of employees (Griffin *et al.*, 2005).

In summary, the findings we have discussed thus far are mixed at best. If the numbers are taken as an indicator, it appears that, overall, feminism has had a positive impact in terms of bringing women, including women of color, into the criminal justice and legal professions. But the numbers belie the extent of true equality – among women and men, people of color and whites, LGBT people and heterosexuals – in these fields. A closer look at what happens once women, people of color, and LGBT people enter these occupations indicates that the feminist goal of progressive social change remains as yet unrealized. As criminologist Marie Griffin (2013: 282) asks, "A foot in the door . . . now what?"

THE FUTURE OF FEMINIST CRIMINOLOGY

The title for this, the final section of the book, was inspired by a volume edited by Rolf Loeber and Brandon Welsh (2012) entitled, *The Future of Criminology*. We would have been pleased if that title was suitable here, but it is impossible to deny that feminist criminology remains on the margins of mainstream criminology. Consider, for example, that in Loeber and Welsh's book, the contents of which are billed as "the field's leading scholars [providing] their views into the future of what needs to be done in research, policy, and practice in the discipline" (see www.oup.com/us/catalog/), the phrase *feminist criminology* appears in none of the 33 chapter titles. The index has entries for "female offending," "gender-specific intervention programs," and "women, offending by" – all of which direct the reader to p. 136, where in one three-sentence paragraph on desistance research, the author notes the need for more studies, especially longitudinal studies, of female offending (Kazemian, 2012). There are no entries for "gender," "feminist criminology," "sexual assault," or any type of violence against women. In a chapter on the implications of brain violence research (Rivara, 2012), the author cites a Washington State study that compares men's and women's reported experiences of childhood sexual abuse. In short, if one uses this book as a guide, criminal offending and victimization remain degendered phenomena and the future of criminology does not include feminist criminology.

Similarly, a brochure advertising the 2012 Annual Robina Institute Conference on "Crime and Justice in America, 1975–2025" at the University of Minnesota Law School, extended the invitation to "join us in a look at the development of criminal justice research and policy in the United States." One opens the brochure to find that the "nine internationally prominent scholars" who will be discussing "how and why policies and research have evolved as they have, what has been learned, and what the implications of that knowledge are for the future," are all white men, none of whom use the words "feminist" or "gender" in describing their research or expertise (Robina Institute of Criminal Law and Criminal Justice, 2012).[10]

Such evidence is, of course, superficial, but I do think it is at least symptomatic of the continuing marginalization of feminist criminology within the discipline as a whole. There are those – including some feminist criminologists – who maintain that feminist criminologists have engaged in self-marginalization by, for instance, establishing separate divisions within professional associations and founding feminist journals.[11] This argument, though, strikes me as hollow in light of the fact that the development of feminist criminology, as we have seen throughout this book, was prompted by the historical neglect of gender – other than using sex as a control variable – in criminological research, and the exclusion of women from academic criminology and the criminal justice professions. Given that this exclusion was followed by marginalization within the discipline and the professions, actions such as establishing feminist journals and sections within disciplinary and professional organizations hardly constitute self-marginalization. Rather, they are strategies for surviving and thriving, and they are a means to give voice and visibility to significant – and, at times, groundbreaking – ideas and research.

Feminist criminologists have broken down, or at least cracked, some of the major barriers erected by the "malestream." In 2012, for instance, the membership of the American Society of Criminology elected Joanne Belknap as their president, and Karen Heimer as their vice president – the first time in ASC history that both the president and the vice president were women, members of the Division on Women and Crime, and feminists. Such developments often lead to further progressive change, albeit not at the rate perhaps that many feminist criminologists would prefer. But while some changes may be slow, the rate of feminist criminological knowledge production is not. The research cited in this slim volume is only a small fraction of the work in which feminist criminologists are engaged. And there are numerous areas yet to be mined from a feminist criminological perspective. Among those that I would like to see feminist criminologists explore in future studies are:

- *Gender-specific criminal justice programming* – We have seen throughout this book that equality versus difference has been a focal point of many debates among feminist (and non-feminist) criminologists. One area in which this issue has arisen with particular intensity is correctional interventions. There are those who point to research showing that female offenders are less dangerous than male offenders; that they typically have a history of victimization, including child sexual abuse and other violent victimization; that many have multiple physical and mental health problems; that most are the primary caregivers to young children; and that they react to imprisonment differently than men do. Consequently, according to this position, female offenders deserve to be treated differently; strategies for dealing with female offenders should be *gender-responsive*, targeting the unique needs and vulnerabilities of women and girls. As Daly (1994: 270) stressed nearly 20 years ago with regard to gender differences in sentencing, "Allowing for gender-linked criteria is not the same as assuming that men's and women's natures differ. . . . It is to assume that some features of men's and women's lives may differ and ought to be acknowledged . . ."

There are, however, several countervailing perspectives. As Bosworth and Fili (2013: 233) point out, for example, "privileging difference" in these ways overlooks the complex intersections of gender, race, and other socially constructed categories of inequality and domination as they relate to crime, correctional intervention, and punishment. They are also concerned that "representing women as a special case" – i.e. as weak, vulnerable, malleable – reinforces paternalism, or worse, justifies underservicing women's correctional facilities and programs, over-medicating women under correctional supervision, and punishing women for minor infractions that would be ignored if committed by men.

Rigorous empirical evaluation of gender-specific programs, including those for battered women who have been mandated by the court for "batterer intervention" services, are badly needed. Merry Morash's (2010) recent research on gender-specific probation and parole programs provides a solid foundation on which to build. Morash emphasizes, though, that gender-responsive community corrections programs are "not a replacement for public policies to prevent and ameliorate" problems, such as child sexual abuse and domestic violence, resulting from structural gender inequality (p. 151). Moreover, Morash's research demonstrated that the wraparound services and continuum of care in the programs she studied are keys to their success (i.e. desistance from crime). But as Bosworth and Fili (2013) point out, features such as these would also be beneficial to male offenders in the correctional system "many of whom [like female offenders] are also non-violent drug offenders, disproportionately drawn from minority communities, with children on the outside, and so forth" (pp. 233–4). Bosworth and Fili are also critical of how the term, "gender-responsive," has been so loosely applied. In fact, they are concerned that given the lack of clarity in defining just what is meant by "gender-responsive" programs and strategies, the term can be – and is – used to legitimate correctional interventions, when one of our goals should be to reduce such interventions and to develop alternatives.

- *Restorative justice options* – One rather controversial alternative to traditional criminal justice interventions is restorative justice. Again, however, this is an area where there is disagreement even with regard to definitions. Susan Miller (2011) makes a useful distinction between diversionary restorative justice programs and therapeutic restorative justice programs. As the name implies, diversionary restorative justice programs divert offenders from the formal legal system, responding to certain types of crimes in community settings instead. The goals of these programs are to overcome the systemic biases of the official criminal justice system, while improving rehabilitative outcomes for offenders and facilitating reconciliation between them and their victims and communities. Such programs use community supervision and often some form of restitution, while allowing offenders to avoid incarceration. Miller characterizes diversionary restorative justice programs as offender-centered. In contrast, therapeutic restorative justice programs are available after an offender has been convicted; they do not replace formal legal adjudication, nor do they substitute community corrections for harsher punishment, including incarceration. Rather, therapeutic restorative justice programs focus on "repairing harm done to victims and facilitat[ing] offenders' accountability while including healing and its potential for people and relationships affected by the crime" (ibid.: 11). The goal is not to reconcile the victim and the offender, but to empower victims and help them recover from their traumatic victimization experiences. Consequently, Miller characterizes therapeutic restorative justice programs as victim-centered.[12]

Concerns have been voiced about using restorative justice in cases involving gendered violence – that is, cases in which the majority of offenders are men and boys, and the majority of victims are women and girls – such as intimate partner violence, child sexual abuse, and stranger and acquaintance rape. Critics of using restorative justice to address such crimes worry that restorative justice programs, especially diversionary programs, do not adequately hold perpetrators accountable for their harmful actions and do nothing to redress the imbalance of power between offenders and victims in these crimes. By failing to sufficiently punish offenders and trying to mediate their relationships with their victims, critics warn that restorative justice programs may expose women and children to increased risk of revictimization.[13]

Miller (2011) argues that these criticisms apply to diversionary restorative justice, but not to therapeutic restorative justice, since the latter is "healing driven, rather than outcome driven," and because therapeutic programs "are not offered at the beginning phase of the criminal justice process, nor are they in lieu of harsher punishment" (p. 13). But what Miller's focus on therapeutic restorative justice overlooks is the disillusionment of some feminists with traditional criminal justice practices in terms of preventing violence against women and children. Reforms in criminal justice responses to sexual assault, intimate partner violence, and other common forms of violence against women have unquestionably improved the well-being of countless women and girls; no doubt, many lives have been saved. But women in most industrialized, high-income countries throughout the world still do not feel safe (Crabtree and Nsubuga, 2012), and some groups of women are reluctant or averse to seeking help from criminal justice authorities. As we discussed in Chapters 3 and 4, the criminal justice system in most Western societies has been especially punitive toward specific groups of men: poor and working-class men, and men in immigrant communities and communities of color. Women from these socially and economically marginalized groups sometimes do not want official legal intervention when they are victimized, because they do not want the men in their communities harshly punished – even if "therapeutic" programs may follow (Goodmark, 2012; Ptacek, 2010b). Therefore, it is incumbent on feminist criminologists, in partnership with marginalized communities, to develop and rigorously evaluate alternative models of protection, accountability, and justice, including various forms of restorative justice.

- *State crime* – The foregoing discussion reminds us not to lose sight of the fact that the State may not be a purveyor of justice, but instead may perpetrate widespread and cruel injustices. DeKeseredy and Dragiewicz (2013) point out that although critical criminologists have conducted a good deal of research on government or state crimes, there are few feminist analyses of these crimes. Feminist research on state crime has been growing over the past 25 years, with the majority of this work focusing on state-sanctioned violence against women, especially violence against women during conflict and war, or violence against women as a result of or in the aftermath of conflict, war, or natural disasters (see, for example, Lee-Koo, 2011; St. Germain and Dewey, 2012; True, 2012). Some researchers have also examined State and international political responses to such violence (for instance, see Borer, 2009; Henry, 2010; Lee-Koo, 2011). Collectively, this work demonstrates that experiences of conflict and war, as well as experiences of peace and security, are, like all aspects of social life, *gendered*. To ignore this fact is perilous for everyone, since if women's victimization experiences are downplayed, disregarded, or excluded from the peacemaking, reconciliation, or rebuilding processes, an effective, equitable, and lasting peace is unlikely (Renzetti, 2011b). But as Kuehnast *et al.*, (2011) show, even when states officially recognize the need for incorporating women's experiences in peacemaking and conflict resolution processes, women's actual participation is hardly guaranteed. The contributors to their volume, for example, analyze United Nations Security Resolutions 1325, 1820, 1888, and 1889, which are designed to protect women from sexual abuse during conflicts, in the post-conflict period, and in refugee camps, as well as to include women in official peacemaking and conflict resolution bodies and activities. A recurring theme in these analyses, however, is the disparity between the written resolutions and their implementation; there are no time-bound targets for achieving stated goals, little or no funding allocated or personnel assigned to work directly on implementation, and perhaps most troubling, no accountability or sanctions for implementation failure or for noncompliance with any of the resolutions' provisions. This is not to say that such efforts are unimportant, but rather to emphasize that they are often largely *symbolic* and considerably more social action and political pressure are needed to get them translated into *practice*.

Attention to women's involvement in peacemaking and conflict resolution also alerts us to the need for feminist analyses not only of women as victims of state crime, but also women as active social agents (DeKeseredy and Dragiewicz, 2013). Consider, for instance, that today there are more women on active military duty and peacekeeping forces than ever before. Many NATO countries now permit women to participate in all areas of their armed forces, including most combat roles, with few exceptions (CBC News Online, 2006). The impact of women's growing involvement as military agents, particularly as active combatants, has yet to be empirically assessed. Some analysts maintain that female peacekeeping troops are more likely than male peacekeepers to use non-confrontational conflict resolution techniques and are trusted more by women in the areas to which they are deployed (ibid.). It is also argued that the presence of female peacekeepers helps to reduce sexual misconduct by male peacekeeping troops (Kuehnast *et al.*, 2011). But such findings are based almost exclusively on anecdotal evidence. A more serious concern, too, is that these arguments contain the familiar ring of essentialism – that is, the notion that women's "natural" or socially produced "goodness," non-aggressiveness, and "higher morality" will reduce tensions in conflict zones, induce men to behave themselves, and make local women safer. This view, though, overlooks the tremendous diversity among women as well as the fact that female military personnel receive the same training as male personnel and they are expected to embrace the same military culture to be successful. It appears naïve at best to assume that simply enlisting more women as peacekeepers and soldiers without changing the hegemonic masculine culture of military organizations will automatically produce more positive outcomes for local citizens and for women peacekeepers and combatants themselves (Callahan, 2009; Renzetti, 2011b). Lest we forget, women military guards participated in the torture and abuse of prisoners at Abu Ghraib.

In studying state crime, therefore, feminist criminologists must examine women as perpetrators as well as victims. Moreover, feminist criminologists, as leaders in research on the intersection of women's victimization and perpetration, should study female soldiers' and peacekeepers' experiences of sexual harassment and assault. For one thing, the societies to which peacekeepers and soldiers are deployed are often highly patriarchal and women hold low status (Kuehnast *et al.*, 2011). Such conditions may put women peacekeepers and soldiers at risk of victimization by local men. In addition, they may be victimized by male fellow peacekeepers and soldiers. For example, reports of the sexual harassment and assault of women at U.S. military academies and on active duty are widespread. In fact, charges of sexual abuse have increased in all branches of the U.S. armed forces, although many military women who are victimized do not file formal complaints because they believe doing so will jeopardize their military careers (Callahan, 2009; Sadler *et al.*, 2000). Even when formal complaints are made, however, few accused perpetrators are brought to trial and fewer still are convicted (General Accounting Office, 2011; Myers, 2009). The consequences for victims nevertheless appear severe and long term, and deserve further empirical investigation (Sadler *et al.*, 2000).

A related area in need of feminist analysis is terrorism (i.e. politically motivated violence and aggression). As Boots and Wareham (2013: 170) note, "Stereotypically, terrorists are thought of as male perpetrators; however, women and girls have consistently been involved in acts of political violence." While some maintain that women become involved in terrorist activities because they are coerced by or "under the spell" of male intimate partners or charismatic leaders, there is evidence that some female terrorists are motivated by the same reasons as male terrorists: political ideology, nationalism, religious beliefs and devotion, perceived resistance to oppression, revenge (Berko *et al.*, 2010). Moreover, while the extent and scope of female involvement in terrorism undoutedly varies, the few researchers who have studied it report that many women assume more than simply supportive roles, establishing themselves in terrorist organizations as soldiers, killers, and martyrs (Berko *et al.*, 2010; Eager, 2008; Gonzalez-Perez, 2008). As one observer phrased it, "The meager evidence we have from the performance of women in espionage and sabotage suggests that women can be as brave and as coldly homicidal as men, whenever their patriotism calls for it" (Quester, 1982: 229). Certainly, this is a type of violent, political, and often state-sponsored crime that warrants the attention of feminist criminologists.

- *Globalization* – This discussion of state crime, especially in the context of war and conflict, raises another significant issue: the need to globalize feminist criminology. Arguably, since the turn of the twenty-first century there has been burgeoning interest in global women's issues, particularly the concerns and experiences of women in non-Western and developing societies. But to paraphrase ethicist Kathy Rudy (2000), this interest has brought Western feminism to a crisis point as Western feminists come to realize the limits of their scholarship for understanding differences across cultural and national borders. Criminologist Rosemary Barberet (forthcoming) identifies several ways these limitations manifest in Western feminist criminological scholarship. First, Western feminist criminology examines the relationship between social class and crime and victimization, but an international analysis requires attention to issues related to socioeconomic development and inequality among countries (see also True, 2012). Second, Western feminist criminology studies racial and ethnic differences in women's experiences of crime and the criminal justice system, whereas an international analysis broadens intersectionality to include gendered experiences of colonization, and expands the types of crimes studied to human rights violations, including human trafficking, the "maid trade" and other gendered forms of labor and financial exploitation (see also ibid.). And third, while Western feminist criminology looks at the gendered ways local police, courts, and correctional institutions respond to offending and victimization, an international analysis of these institutional responses includes such bodies as the United Nations, the International Criminal Court, truth commissions and war crimes tribunals, and transnational civil society organizations (see also Borer, 2009; Henry, 2010; St. Germain and Dewey, 2012).

Not surprisingly, those who advocate the globalization of feminist criminology are at the same time concerned with the problems that arise when one exports Western theories to non-Western societies. As Rudy (2000: 1051) points out, imposing "any metanarrative that seeks to describe otherness in Western terms (such as the human rights discourse associated with liberalism, the essentialism of radical feminism, or the materiality embedded in orthodox Marxism) . . . functions as another form of colonization." Thus, while embracing globalization as a worthy goal, Western feminist criminologists are faced with daunting questions:

> How can we inquire about practices that are foreign to us in ways that capture some of the complexities involved in different constructions of reality? How can we step outside our assumptions and view our own lives through the lens of another? If women across cultural and national borders have little in common, how can we organize together against oppression? How can we be sensitive to difference and politically progressive at the same time?
>
> (Rudy, 2000: 1051)

These are questions that we addressed in part in Chapter 4 when we considered critiques of postmodern feminist criminology. This book itself is a partial response to these questions in that it shows feminism to be not a single, unified theory, but rather "a loosely organized set of theories, convictions, and practices" (Rudy, 2000: 1052). Recognition of this fact encourages us to begin any analysis of crime and justice in other societies by interrogating our own cultural values, assumptions, principles and politics (Barberet, forthcoming; Rudy, 2000) and by taking seriously critiques of Western feminism by non-Western feminists. As Collins (1986) pointed out, the limitations and errors of a particular perspective can be best identified and understood by "outsiders within." But as we also emphasized in Chapter 4, this does not mean that it is impossible for Western feminist criminologists to develop an understanding of non-Western women's experiences of crime and justice or that "local constructions of reality are always better and should remain uninfected by Western theories" (Rudy, 2000: 1053). Rather, Western feminist criminologists must be willing to engage with non-Western feminist criminologists in an exchange of ideas and analyses of diverse women's experiences of crime and justice, accepting that often an indigenous perspective may be more accurate and may offer the most appropriate and effective solutions to a problem. As Rudy (ibid.) wisely observes, "Such a posture allows us, in short, to pay attention to difference, without leading us down the path to indifference."

I am certain that readers of this book could offer many more suggestions to this list. I have more recommendations myself, but these four reflect my *personal* priorities for the future of feminist criminology, with the caveat that I do not presume these are the only or the most important areas for exploration. It is not likely that pursuing any of these recommendations will result in feminist criminology being welcomed into the "mainstream" of the discipline, but I find this prospect less troubling than I used to. For one thing, I frankly do not want to be "one of the boys." In addition, however, I am indebted to criminologist Pat Carlen (2011: 99) for exhorting against evangelism in criminology and in favor of criminology as a scientific art. Carlen points to the tendency of some "brand-name criminologies" to market themselves in opposition to "mainstream" or "conventional" criminology, to "call others to join them in various types of 'activism,'" and to be "overly prescriptive" about what types of research or theorizing constitute significant contributions to the enterprise. She opposes this evangelizing, first, because she correctly sees it as grounded in "oppositional rhetoric rather than creative analysis," and, therefore, "antagonistic to scientific endeavor" (p. 101). But second, she opposes it because it distracts criminologists from doing their jobs – "[f]or there are all kinds of jobs to be done by criminologists and there are many different ways of doing them" (p. 106) – by focusing their energies on being "some kind of partisan criminologist" (p. 101). Instead, she maintains that "because criminology is a science, it should be: open; constantly recognizing, questioning, and, if necessary, destroying the conditions of its own existence; and neither 'trimming' its questions to make them politically correct or expedient, nor 'clubbing' – that is, pulling its punches – either to conform to contemporary academic fashions or political prejudices, or in response to disciplinary bullying by either political or academic powers-that-be" (Carlen, 2011: 97).

Carlen's argument leads us back to the position raised in our discussion of globalization: to avoid imposing metanarratives; to begin by interrogating our own values, assumptions, principles and politics; to take seriously the critiques of the "outsiders within"; and to engage in a respectful exchange of ideas. But I am applying this position to feminist criminology itself, for as we have emphasized throughout this book, feminist criminology is a diverse collection of theoretical perspectives and methods. So to paraphrase Carlen (2011: 105), instead of wasting our precious time and energy on establishing ourselves in opposition to "mainstream" criminology and discerning whether or not those among us are feminist "enough" or the "right kind" of feminist, it would be more productive to "concentrate on doing a good job in terms of fulfilling a desired object of research – which might well be pure, political, or campaigning research and conducted according to any one of an unlimited range of transparent research methods."[14]

There is some evangelizing in this book, to be sure; if I am totally honest, I find it impossible to overcome my feminist – in the broadest sense of the term – partisanship. But at the end of the day, my hope is that readers take from the book a fuller understanding of the diverse perspectives and methods that are feminist criminology and find them useful for doing their jobs as students of criminology and as criminologists – whatever those jobs may be.

Notes

1 Feminist criminology: a brief overview

1 Offen (1988: 124) points out that European feminists, much more so than American feminists, "celebrated sexual difference rather than similarity within a framework of male/female complementarity; and instead of seeking unqualified admission to male-dominated society, they mounted a widespread critique of the society and its institutions."

2 The categories "male" and "female" as well as "masculinity" and "femininity" are typically thought of as not only homogenous, but also as binary or dichotomous. Research, however, indicates that they are neither. Individuals who are intersexed, for example, have ambiguous genitalia and may have internal sex organs that do not "match" the sex of their external genitalia (Preves, 2003). There are, moreover, numerous ways to "do" masculinity and femininity, as outlined in Chapter 4, and these vary not only across individuals, but also by the same individual in different social settings.

3 Notice, too, that feminist researchers typically use the term research "participants," rather than research "subjects," to refer to those people who they study. This is related to the principle of reciprocity in that research should not be something that is "done to" those who agree to be studied. The research process establishes a relationship between the researcher and the researched in which those researched give the researcher their time and information and the researcher, in turn, should give something back to those they research. Researchers who use a feminist participatory model take the term research "participants" a step further by inviting those who they are studying to be collaborators on the project – e.g. helping to design and implement the project as well as disseminate the findings. See, for instance, Renzetti (1997); see also Jaffe *et al.* (2011).

2 Liberal feminist criminology

1 Lombroso, for instance, maintained that all women are less evolved than men, which resulted in them having certain "primitive" traits. Women, according to Lombroso, are naturally vengeful and jealous; their moral sensibilities are deficient; and they are less sensitive to pain than men. In the majority of women, these defects are neutralized by other feminine traits that Lombroso viewed more positively:

passivity, physical weakness, low intelligence, and a maternal "instinct." Obviously, Lombroso did not have a high opinion even of conforming women. In the criminal woman, though, the "bad qualities" of women are intensified, and there are no "maternal sentiments" to counteract them. Instead, there are "strong passions and intensely erotic tendencies, much muscular strength and a superior intelligence for the conception and execution of evil," which makes such women, in Lombroso's view, "more terrible than any man" (Lombroso and Ferrero, 1893: 150).

2 Christine Rasche (1974) has pointed out that this argument is not a novel one, citing Bishop (1931), who blamed the "liberation" of women in the 1920s for an increase in female offending.

3 Indeed, Adler (1975) offers numerous quotes from female offenders who "identify with a value code embracing the 'traditional' image of women," and who associate feminism with "lesbians" and "kooks." These women scoff "at the mention of any connection between [their] latest criminal actions and the beliefs of the female emancipation movement" (Adler, 1975: 7–8).

4 Some feminist criminologists refuse to label emancipation theory and work in this vein "feminist." Gelsthorpe and Morris (1988: 227), for instance, write that they do not describe Adler's and Simon's work as feminist because "it does not contain certain core elements" that feminist criminology comprises, including those presented in Chapter 1 of this book. Similarly, Simpson (1989: 610, fn. 5) cites Leonard (1982) when she remarks that a "research focus on gender alone does not qualify one as a feminist just as a focus on class does not make one a Marxist." For research and theorizing to be feminist, as we emphasized in Chapter 1, the criminologist must examine gender *relations* as well as the unique consequences of patriarchal oppression.

5 Although she acknowledges the positive contributions of Adler's and Simon's work, Sally Simpson (1989: 610) emphasizes its negative impact. She points out that both Klein (1973) in the U.S. and Smart (1976) in the U.K. had "set an agenda for a new feminist criminology" that was far more radical than liberal feminism, focusing on gendered economic and social inequalities as the causes of female offending, and on patriarchy to explain the sexist treatment of women in the criminal justice system. This agenda, however, was "derailed" by the publication of Adler's and Simon's books, both of which essentially served to fuel the backlash against the feminist movement (see also Chesney-Lind, 1980; Smart, 1976). Nicole Rafter (2000) also notes the contributions of Frances Heidensohn (1968) in Britain and Marie-Andree Bertrand (1967) in Canada, who challenged criminology's androcentrism and laid the foundation for feminist criminology several years before Adler's and Simon's books were published.

6 Interestingly, one consequence of the global economic recession that began in 2007 has been an increase in families in which the female partner is in the paid labor force and the male partner is unemployed

or underemployed. Although the economic recession has hurt both women and men, men have lost more jobs more quickly than women have since 2007 (Rampell, 2010). Thus, more women are becoming the sole breadwinners for their families. Although it remains to be seen how this change will impact marital power relations in the long term, there is research showing that in some families such a shift – from male as primary breadwinner to female as primary breadwinner – does not necessarily lead to greater power for women in the marriage, but instead generates marital conflict, particularly when men who adhere to traditional patriarchal gender norms feel that their masculinity is being undermined and their dominance is eroding (Grzywacz *et al.*, 2009; Kaukinen, 2004; MacMillan and Gartner, 1999; Raj *et al.*, 1999; Renzetti, 2011a).

7 Adler's (1997) brief history, published in the ASC's newsletter, *The Criminologist*, makes for interesting reading. She reports, for example, that in the 1930s, a group of August Vollmer's graduate students used to meet informally to talk about police administration. They used to wear lapel pins with a V etched in the center, representing the name they had given themselves: the V-Men (Vollmer-Men), a moniker that leaves no doubt as to the male exclusivity of the club.

8 Adler (1997) notes parenthetically that Harvard Law School denied Eleanor Glueck a professorship, a position held by her husband, Sheldon Glueck. She was instead a senior research scholar with her work tied to that of her husband.

9 Like Garrison and her colleagues (1992), I also found that many faculty members do not regard course content about women specifically, and gender more broadly, as central or necessary to what they teach. In a survey of faculty at the institution where I was working in the early 1980s, I asked my colleagues if they incorporated women's experiences and perspectives into their courses. The near-unanimous response was, "Only when they're relevant." I am still struck by the fact that the ideas and experiences of half of humanity could be cavalierly dismissed as unimportant or peripheral to the "real" knowledge to be imparted in a course.

10 Scarborough (2000) discusses the case of *Griggs v. Duke Power Co.* (1971) in which the U.S. Supreme Court ruled that a plaintiff does not have to prove that an employer intentionally discriminated, but only that job qualifications exclude a certain group or class of citizens – for example, women. The employer then has to prove that these qualifications are essential to the job and no other means of selecting employees could be used. This ruling, which became known as the *Griggs* standard, was subsequently instrumental in striking down minimum height and weight requirements and specific physical agility tests that had been used for years as the basis for excluding women from policing and as correctional officers. The courts ruled that such "qualifications" were unrelated to job

performance and therefore could not be used as a condition for hiring (Belknap, 2001; Scarborough, 2000; Stohr, 2006).

11 Heidensohn (2000) acknowledges similarities between the history of women police officers in Britain and that of their sisters in the U.S., but also notes important differences, including the self-image of British policewomen as professional police officers, not as social workers.

12 The increase in women attorneys enlarged the pool of women eligible for judicial appointments. Nevertheless, women's judicial appointments occurred far more slowly than their entry into the legal profession. In the U.S., for example, "there was a lapse of about 50 years between when the first woman was admitted to the bar in the state and the first woman was appointed to the bench" (Meloy *et al.*, 2006: 240–1). There were women judges as early as the 1920s and 1930s, but "it wasn't until 1979 that a woman had served at some level of the judicial system in all 50 states" (Meloy *et al.*, 2006: 241). By 1985, in the U.S., women were about 6.8 percent of state judges and 10.7 percent of federal judges (not including U.S. Supreme Court justices) (Renzetti and Curran, 1989).

3 The subordination of women

1 Some criminologists have looked at gender differences in the effects of labeling. For example, Bartusch and Matsueda (1996) found that boys who were labeled rule breakers by their parents tended to come to see themselves as delinquents and subsequently engage in more rule breaking, which is what labeling theorists would predict. However, girls in this study who were labeled rule breakers by their parents tended to stop engaging in rule breaking in an effort to try to please their parents, a finding that highlights the importance of empirically testing a theory using a sample that includes males *and* females. There is also a substantial body of research that examines gender differences in responses to offending by the police and the courts. Although not undertaken by labeling theorists, such studies are relevant to labeling theorists' concern with status degradation ceremonies and their outcomes. We examine this research later in the chapter.

2 For example, Marx, along with his friend and fellow revolutionary, Frederick Engels, considered criminals members of the "lumpenproletariat," that is, "the 'dangerous class,' the social scum, the passively rotting mass thrown off by the lowest layers of the old society . . ." (Marx and Engels, 1948: 20). Elsewhere, though, Marx and Engels discussed some crime as a form of revolt against the ruling class and the capitalist system (Engels, 1845), and also as a product of the demoralization or brutalization of working class life under industrial capitalism (Cain and Hunt, 1979). These latter two views were influential in the work of contemporary critical criminology.

3 Consider, for instance, recent statistics showing that in nearly two-thirds (64 percent) of violent crimes committed against women, the victim knew her assailant, whereas in only 40 percent of violent crimes against men did the victim know his assailant (Truman, 2011). These gender differences are fairly consistent over time. See, for example, Craven (1996) and Kruttschnitt (2001).

4 Some criminologists have argued for greater attention to the ways in which victimization by corporate crime is gendered. For example, Gerber and Weeks (1992) point out that women have always been victims of corporate crime; indeed, in cases such as the Dalkon Shield contraceptive device and faulty silicone breast implants, women were the only victims of such crimes. Most criminologists, though, continue to overlook gender in their studies of corporate crime. For exceptions, see Baker (2001); Dodge (2013); Dodge and Geis (2003); and Rynbrandt and Kramer (1995).

5 Although the media have given considerable attention to the progress women have made in recent years in terms of assuming leadership positions in government and business, they remain underrepresented in positions of power (Kellerman and Rhode, 2007). For instance, fewer than 3 percent of Fortune 500 chief executive officers (CEOs) are women (Scherer, 2010; Soares *et al.*, 2010). Worldwide, in countries with parliamentary governments – that is, 189 countries – women held just 18.4 percent of the seats in 2008. Granted, this is a 600 percent increase since 1945 – although the number of parliaments has also grown during this period from 26 to 189 – but it can hardly be seen as "revolutionary" or as affording women the same opportunities, legitimate or otherwise, that men have. Relative to these 189 countries, the U.S. ranks seventy-first, despite the fact that women have made considerable progress in political office-holding at all levels since the 1990s (Inter-Parliamentary Union, 2008a, 2008b). For a comprehensive discussion of women's involvement in white-collar crime, however, see Dodge (2009, 2013).

6 In the late 1990s, both women's and men's arrests for larceny-theft declined significantly, which many criminologists attributed to the low unemployment rate and the healthy economy (see, for example, Fagan and Freeman, 1999). However, since the start of the most recent economic recession in late 2007, women's arrests for larceny theft have gone up, while men's arrests for this crime have continued to go down. While some argue that this may reflect women's greater economic marginalization, it is the case that men have been losing jobs at a faster rate than women. Nevertheless, women who are poor, whom we have already identified as disproportionately represented among those arrested and incarcerated, are especially likely to have been hard hit by the economic downturn. This is certainly an issue that deserves the attention of criminologists.

7 Sexual Assault Nurse Examiner (SANE) programs involve the use of specially trained nurses to provide comprehensive care, including

medical, psychological, and forensic services, to sexual assault victims in hospital emergency departments, instead of these services being provided by an emergency room physician. Research indicates that SANE programs contribute to reduced sexual assault case attrition in the criminal justice system and improve post-assault care for victims (Campbell *et al.*, 2011, 2012). Recounting the history of the anti-violence against women movement is beyond the scope of this book, but several excellent comprehensive histories are available; see Caringella (2008), Pleck (1987), and Schechter (1982).

8 Take Back the Night (also called Reclaim the Night) marches and related activities are intended to raise community awareness about the problem of violence against women and to express commitment toward working to end all forms of gender-based violence. The first Take Back the Night candlelight street procession is thought to have occurred in Philadelphia, PA in 1975. In 1976, during the International Tribunal on Crimes against Women convened in Brussels, Belgium, an estimated 2,000 women from 40 countries also participated in a candlelight street procession. Since that time, similar "Shine Your Light" walks have been held annually in countries throughout the world, usually during the months of April or October. For more information, consult www.takebackthenight.org. Training curricula on prevention of and interventions for sexual assault, intimate partner violence, dating violence, and other forms of gender-based violence are available from a variety of organizations, including End Violence against Women International (EVAWI; www/evawintl.org), Domestic Abuse Intervention Programs (DAIP; www.theduluthmodel.org), and Green Dot, etc. (www.livethegreen dot.com).

9 It must be noted that the feminist critiques of Marxist, radical and socialist feminist criminologies are significantly different from those of backlash critics, who argue that feminists exaggerate the prevalence of violence against women while understating or deliberately hiding women's use of violence in intimate relationships (see, for example, Dutton, 2006; Sommers, 1995, 2012; Straus, 2007). These arguments will not be addressed here; the fallacies and distortions inherent in them have been ably addressed by others. See, for instance, DeKeseredy (2011a) and Dragiewicz (2011).

10 The unintended, but harmful consequences of this characterization become clear when women physically fight back against an abusive intimate partner, which also highlights the intersection between victimization and offending in many women's lives. For example, in the U.S. every state now has some form of mandatory or pro-arrest policy in place for police to follow in responding to intimate partner violence calls. These have resulted in dramatic increases in the number of *women* arrested on assault and domestic violence charges, even though they may have been acting in self-defense, out of frustration from not being able to escape or end the abusive

relationship, or to assert themselves in the face of an abusive partner's controlling behavior (Dasgupta, 2002; Larance and Dasgupta, 2012; Miller, 2005; Stark, 2007). In court, the stereotype of the "real" battered woman as passive and helpless, suffering from "Battered Woman Syndrome," works against women who have actively resisted abuse (Ferraro, 2003, 2006; Randall, 2004; U.S. Department of Justice and U.S. Department of Health and Human Services, 1996). For additional research regarding women's resistance to abuse and coercive control, see Cermele (2010), Hollander (2009), Jordan (2005), and Wesely and Wright (2009).

11 Some observers have argued that essentializing women's experiences with regard to violent victimization was instrumental in getting politicians as well as the (white) general public to pay closer attention and move the issue of violence against women to the national policy agenda. Claiming that *all* women were potential victims sent the message that this was not a problem affecting only poor women or women of color (read, powerless women), but also white, middle-class women (Fedders, 1997; Goodmark, 2012; Richie, 2005, 2012).

4 Identities and intersectionalities

1 Although the doing gender/doing difference approach is widely used – and, according to its creators (West and Zimmerman, 2009), often misused – today, West and Zimmerman persevered for ten years (through multiple revisions) to get their paper accepted for publication, a fact of which up-and-coming theorists and authors in particular should take note.

2 The label "third-wave feminism" is often applied to the feminism of many young women today to set it apart from the feminism of the 1960s, 1970s, and 1980s, which has been referred to as the "second wave of feminism," distinguishing it from late eighteenth- and early nineteenth-century feminism (i.e. the "first wave") (Renzetti *et al.*, 2012). Third wave feminism is commonly described as rebellious in terms of its celebration of female sexuality, and its emphasis on women's autonomy and agency (Lorber, 2005, 2009). An important element of third-wave feminism is inclusion. Many third-wave feminists have developed a multiracial/multicultural worldview focusing on the consequences of racism, social class inequality, and homophobia in addition to sexism (Baumgardner and Richards, 2000; Renzetti *et al.*, 2012). We discuss this perspective in greater detail later in the chapter.

3 See also Goodey's (1997) analysis of masculinities and fear of crime and Miller's (1998) study of gender and the accomplishment of robbery in the U.S., as well as Brookman *et al.*'s (2007) study of gender and robbery in the UK. Stroud (2012) offers a fascinating analysis of how carrying concealed handguns helps "relatively privileged men" to accomplish hegemonic masculinity "through fantasies of violence and self-defense," especially against racial and ethnic minority men.

4 Here I will highlight only a few of what I consider the most salient criticisms of structured action theory. For a more thorough and nuanced discussion of these criticisms, see the exchange between Miller and Messerschmidt in the November, 2002 issue of *Theoretical Criminology*, which we repeatedly cite in this chapter. See also the symposium on doing gender in the February, 2009 issue of *Gender & Society*; several of the contributions to the symposium are cited in this chapter as well.

5 Once again, the challenge is to recognize that even sex is not a binary category. When we speak of an individual's sex, we may be referring to *chromosomal* sex, *hormonal* sex, *gonadal* sex, or *genital* sex. Although for many people all of these are consistent with the category male or the category female, for some people they are not. For instance, some individuals (approximately 1 in 5,000 to 1 in 15,000 births) are born with a pair of XX sex chromosomes, which makes them chromosomally female, but because of prenatal exposure to androgens (male sex hormones) their external genitals may look more like those of boys than girls. This is a condition known as congenital adrenal hyperplasia. Similarly, some fetuses with male sex chromosomes (XY) are insensitive to androgens – a condition known as androgen insensitivity syndrome – and they are then born with the external genitalia of females. Typically, physicians advise parents of children with these conditions to have their genitals surgically reconstructed or "corrected." But this position has come under increasing criticism because such conditions usually are not threatening to the child's health; as one critic put it, they are only threatening to the child's culture (Kessler, 1996). For further discussion of *intersexuality*, genital ambiguity, and cross-cultural research on multiple genders, see Preves (2003) and Renzetti *et al.* (2012).

6 Stop and frisk refers to the ability of police to stop a person they deem "suspicious" to question them and pat them down (i.e. frisk them) in order to detect weapons. This controversial practice has been challenged as an unconstitutional search, but the U.S. Supreme Court has upheld it as a legitimate way to prevent crime, especially violent crime, and has given police considerable discretion in terms of what they deem "reasonably suspicious." Some people, however, are automatically labeled suspicious because of their membership in a particular group, such as people of color, so they are disproportionately – and unfairly – subjected to this practice. Saturation policing refers to the practice of concentrating large numbers of police officers in small, high-crime areas (known as "hot spots"). The rationale is to have a highly visible and overwhelming police presence in order to deter crime, which, on its face, makes sense. However, the police may be perceived as an "occupying army," particularly in racially segregated and economically disadvantaged neighborhoods. Ironically, some residents of such neighborhoods point out that despite saturation

policing, the police are often quite slow to respond to their calls for help (see, for example, Websdale, 2001). Finally, the three strikes law, adopted in California, was originally intended to reduce the recidivism of violent felons by imposing a life sentence in prison on individuals convicted of a third offense. Most "strike crimes" (i.e. criminal convictions that count in the three-strike tally) are violent felonies, but other, less serious crimes are included as well as are juvenile convictions and out-of-state convictions. The law has resulted in many grossly unfair outcomes (e.g. an individual being sentenced to life in prison for a shoplifting conviction because it was his or her "third strike" while an individual convicted of manslaughter is sentenced to 15 years because it is his or her first conviction). The law has also contributed to the serious – and inhumane – prison overcrowding in California, where one in four inmates is a "striker" (Shouse Law Group, 2012). See also Alexander (2010) for further discussion of these and other, similar practices.

7 As the economic downturn that began in 2007 began to worsen, the media reported an upsurge in cases of domestic violence, both intimate partner violence and child abuse, and attributed the increase to growing depression among men who had recently lost their jobs or who were experiencing severe financial problems. This group included middle-class and wealthy men who had lost positions in high-paying, high-status professions. But while research indicates a strong association between economic hardship and domestic violence, the relationship is complex and, often, economic distress is only one factor that must be considered in conjunction with a host of other risk factors. See Renzetti (2011a) for a further discussion of these issues.

8 Wonders (1999: 112) points out that "some postmodern theorists argue that it is not possible to summarize the field at all, since postmodernism is a response against 'totalizing' theory or efforts to explain the world in a unified and unifying way." Wonders herself maintains that it is unproductive to try to force postmodernism and feminism into a single theory because in doing so one runs the risk of "losing something from each perspective" (ibid.). Rather, she advocates "bridging" the two theories by identifying their "points of convergence."

9 Other terms that have been applied to these intersecting inequalities are "trilogy of oppression" (Gordon, 1987), referring to the disadvantaged status of women of color in terms of gender, race, and class, and "multiple jeopardy" (King, 1988), which encompasses the multiple forms of oppression experienced simultaneously by women of color.

10 We wish to emphasize here that the impact has largely been limited to *feminist* criminology and not the discipline as a whole. As we discuss in Chapter 5, the extent to which feminism generally, or any

specific feminist theory, has influenced the discipline of criminology is debatable.

11 Wood (2012) notes that many abused black women experience additional pressure not to report their violent intimate partners to police in order to "protect" black men from the racist criminal justice system. Wood indicates that this pressure comes from several sources within the black community, such as black clergy who characterize the black male as an "endangered species," and others who send the message that "if you report and/or prosecute your abuser, you are contributing to the problem because black men are stigmatized and 'selectively' over-penalized. In this way, a woman of color may be discouraged from making the choice to protect herself from an abuser by a sense of cultural duty to keep a black man out of the hands of 'white authority figures'" (p. 50). But see also Beth Richie's (2012) excellent analysis of how, over the past two decades, the anti-violence movement, in an effort to win mainstream public support for its cause as well as funding from an increasingly conservative government, abandoned its more radical demands and practices, thereby abandoning women who fall outside hegemonic femininity and heteronormative sexuality – for example, black women in marginalized positions – while at the same time embracing policies, such as mandatory arrest laws, which support what she calls the "prison nation." Her research shows that under these conditions, "the more socially disadvantaged black women are, the more they will be stigmatized by or, worse, punished, for [sic] their victimization" (p. 159).

12 Ransby (2000) offers several excellent examples of black feminists' resistance to women's oppression within the black community. She notes black feminists' protests of Clarence Thomas' nomination to the U.S. Supreme Court in 1991. She also discusses black feminists' rallies against plans by "the predominantly male political establishment" in Harlem (New York City) and St. Louis, Missouri to celebrate boxer Mike Tyson's release from prison after serving his sentence on a rape conviction. And she relates how black feminist law professor Kimberle Creshaw organized a national meeting in 1995 for black feminists to develop responses to Louis Farrakhan's "Million Man March," one of the central purposes of which was to exhort black men to reclaim their rightful titles as heads of their families and communities. As Ransby (2000: 1217) explains, however, "The issue, for many, was not clear cut: for some, opposing Clarence Thomas's sexism had been easy because there were so many other reasons (having to do with his conservative antiblack politics) to oppose him, but to challenge a charismatic religious icon like Farrakhan or a superstar athlete like Tyson was a different matter altogether. Nevertheless, black feminists once again mobilized on fairly short notice to do precisely that."

13 See Muhammad (2010) for a historical analysis of how the association of Blackness with crime has been socially constructed in the United States. In a commentary on Muhammad's book, Kay Harris (2012) observed that the cultural racialization of crime may be summed up in the sentence, "white people commit crimes; black people are criminals."

14 In an interesting analysis of juvenile court decision making, Guevara *et al.* (2006) found that the effect of race on both pre-adjudication detention and case disposition decisions varied by gender, but in different ways. For example, white girls were more likely than non-white girls to receive an out-of-home placement – a harsher disposition and the opposite of what occurred for the boys in the study – which they speculate may reflect the racialized gender stereotypes of juvenile court authorities who regard delinquency by white girls as a more serious violation of gender norms than delinquency by non-white girls. Spohn and Brennan's (2013) discussion of sentencing in capital cases also indicates that racialized gender stereotypes may affect sentencing in capital cases. The studies they review (Holcomb *et al.*, 2004; Williams *et al.*, 2007) showed that offenders convicted of capital crimes against females were two and a half times more likely to be sentenced to death than offenders convicted of capital crimes against males, but when the race of the victim was also examined, the data showed that offenders convicted of killing white females had the greatest likelihood of being sentenced to death, whereas those convicted of killing black males had the lowest likelihood of receiving a death sentence. An offender who killed a white female was 14 times more likely to be sentenced to death than an offender who killed a black male. Factors that further affected the imposition of the death sentence in cases involving white female homicide victims included whether the victim had been raped, whether the victim's body was unclothed when found, and whether there was evidence that the victim had been forced to disrobe.

5 Future directions in feminist criminology

1 Such disagreements are hardly unique to feminist criminology. See, for instance, Howard and Allen (2000), as well as Stacey and Thorne (1996) and the divergent responses from Burawoy (1996) and Smith (1996).

2 The U.S. Department of Education periodically revises the labels it uses to identify various academic majors. In 2008–9, for example, the U.S. Department of Education provided statistics for undergraduate and graduate degree recipients by sex and race for "legal professions and studies," and for "homeland security, law enforcement, and fire fighting." It should be noted, too, that other fields of study that

graduate criminologists, such as public administration and sociology, are also counted separately from the CJ majors by the U.S. Department of Education.

3 Gabbidon *et al.* (2004) report that undergraduate and graduate criminal justice programs have increased in recent years at historically black colleges and universities (HBCUs), which in turn will also increase the number of black faculty and criminal justice professionals.

4 If the lively exchanges on the listserv of the Division on Women and Crime (DWC) of the American Society of Criminology are any indication, there is a great deal of innovation going on in numerous criminology and criminal justice courses being taught by feminist criminologists. DWC members frequently use the listserv to solicit suggestions from fellow members about publications, films, and other ideas and resources for their courses. The DWC web site also provides a list of helpful teaching resources (see www.ascdwc.com).

5 Also relevant here, however, is DeKeseredy and Schwartz's (2010: 161) criticism that some left realist criminologists' attempts to refashion left realism are actually just "more of the same" because this "new" left realism remains gender-blind.

6 Interestingly, historical research shows that in most countries, when women were first permitted to join law enforcement agencies as sworn officers, they were often assigned to "traditional female roles," such as "desk duties" (i.e. clerical work) or interviewing female and child crime victims, constituting essentially, albeit unofficially, a "special" female police unit (DeJong, 2013).

7 Rabe-Hemp (2009) found that female officers who overemphasize their femininity may win more approval from male officers, but their fellow female officers may view such behavior negatively. For a discussion of female officers' efforts to balance their policing careers with pregnancy and motherhood, see Cowan and Bochantin (2009). There is very little research that examines the intersection of inequalities in policing. For studies of racial and ethnic minority officers' policing experiences, see Rojek and Decker (2009) and Thompson (2006). DeJong (2013) also reviews research that examines how the intersection of gender and sexual orientation influences officers' work experiences.

8 According to a 2012 Catalyst report, 1993 was the year of highest percentage enrollment for women in U.S. law schools. Siemsen and Candela (2013) also report that racial and ethnic minority enrollments have declined even more dramatically, although as we see in Table 5.2, in every racial and ethnic group, except for whites, women outnumbered men as law school graduates in 2009–10.

9 There are comparatively few studies of gender and race/ethnicity and judging, but for a review of the extant research, see Siemsen and Candela (2013).

10 Interestingly, however, one speaker's bio makes explicit mention of a longitudinal study he has conducted with 400 males, from age eight into their fifties, and another study of 1,500 males between the ages of 7 and 35.

11 Feminist sections within professional associations include the Women and Crime Division of the American Society of Criminology; the Minorities and Women Section of the Academy of Criminal Justice Sciences; the Gender, Crime and Justice Working Group of the European Society of Criminology; and the Women, Crime and Criminal Justice Network of the British Society of Criminology. Feminist criminological journals include *Feminist Criminology*, *Women and Criminal Justice*, and *Violence Against Women*.

12 Ptacek (2010a) provides a helpful discussion of the history of restorative justice and various types of restorative justice programs.

13 Hudson (1998) extends this critique to racialized violence as well. See Ptacek (2010b) for several insightful analyses of these and other criticisms of restorative justice for responding to violence against women.

14 Feminist sociologist Judith Stacey (2000: 1190–1) notes (with a clear tone of disappointment) that Women's Studies in general has been transformed by institutionalization and professionalization from a "subversive, intellectual arm of a thriving grassroots movement" into an academic discipline with its "own celebrity system" of feminists who "actively participate in the global jet set of an academic commodity market . . ." Stacey laments the fact that many feminist scholars produce work that has no practical purpose, "composed in ungainly prose infused with gratuitous displays of arcane jargon" (p. 1191). To this I would add the unfortunate tendency of some feminist "elites" to trash the work of their "sisters" who they deem not feminist "enough" or the "wrong kind" of feminist. As Stacey (ibid.) observes, "How sobering to note that academic feminist 'sisterhood' has proven powerful enough to replicate many of the less endearing status hierarchies, anxieties, affectations, and schisms of 'normal science.'"

References

Academy of Criminal Justice Sciences (ACJS) (2012) *Certification Standards for College/University Criminal Justice Baccalaureate Degree Programs, 2005*. Retrieved from www.acjs.org/pubs/167_667_12021.cfm.

Adler, F. (1975) *Sisters in Crime*, New York: McGraw-Hill.

—— (1997) "The ASC and women: One generation without, one generation with", *The Criminologist*. Retrieved from http://www/asc41.com/History.html.

Akers, R.L., and Sellers, C.S. (2008) *Criminological Theories*, New York: Oxford University Press.

Alexander, M. (2010) *The New Jim Crow: Mass Incarceration in the Era of Colorblindness*, New York: New Press.

Amato, P.R., and Maynard, R.A. (2007) "Decreasing nonmarital births and strengthening marriage to reduce poverty", *Future of Children*, 2. Retrieved from www.futureofchildren.org.

American Bar Association (2001) *The Unfinished Agenda: Women and the Legal Profession*, Chicago: American Bar Association.

American Bar Association, Commission on Women in the Profession (2006) *Visible Invisibility: Women of Color in Law Firms*, Chicago: American Bar Association.

—— (2008) *From Visible Invisibility to Visibly Successful: Success Strategeies for Law Firms and Women of Color*, Chicago: American Bar Association.

Baca Zinn, M. (2012) "Patricia Hill Collins: Past and future innovations", *Gender & Society*, 26: 28–32.

Baca Zinn, M., Cannon, L.W., Higgenbotham, E., and Thornton Dill, B. (1986) "The cost of exclusionary practices in women's studies", *Signs*, 11: 290–303.

Baca Zinn, M., and Thornton Dill, B. (1996) "Theorizing difference from multiracial feminism", *Feminist Studies*, 22: 321-31.

Baker, L. (2001) "Control and the Dalkon shield", *Violence Against Women*, 7: 1303–17.

Barberet, R. (forthcoming) *Women, Crime and Criminal Justice: A Global Inquiry*, London: Routledge.

Bartusch, D.J., and Matsueda, R.L. (1996) "Gender, reflected appraisals, and labeling: A cross-group test of an interactionist theory of delinquency", *Social Forces*, 75: 145–76.

Baumgardner, J., and Richards, A. (2000) *Manifesta: Young Women, Feminism, and the Future*, New York: Farrar, Straus, and Giroux.

Becker, H.S. (1970) *Sociological Work*, Chicago: Aldine.

—— (1973) *Outsiders*, New York: Free Press.

Belknap, J. (2001) *The Invisible Woman: Gender, Crime, and Justice* (2nd ed.), Belmont, CA: Wadsworth.

Bergen, R.K. (1993) "Interviewing survivors of marital rape: Doing feminist research on sensitive topics", in C.M. Renzetti and R.M. Lee (eds.), *Researching Sensitive Topics*, Newbury Park, CA: SAGE.

Berko, A., Erez, E., and Globokar, J.L. (2010) "Gender, crime and terrorism: The case of Arab/Palestinian women in Israel", *British Journal of Criminology*, 50: 670–89.

Bertrand, M.A. (1967) "The myth of sexual equality before the law", in *Proceedings of the Fifth Research Conference on Delinquency and Criminology*, Montreal: Quebec Society of Criminology.

Bishop, C. (1931) *Women and Crime*, London: Chatto and Windus.

Boba, R., and Lilley, D. (2009) "Violence Against Women Act (VAWA) funding: A nationwide assessment of effects on rape and assault", *Violence Against Women*, 15: 168–85.

Boots, D.P., and Wareham, J. (2013) "A gendered view of violence", in C.M. Renzetti, S.L. Miller, and A.R. Gover (eds.) *Routledge International Handbook of Crime and Gender Studies*, London: Routledge.

Borer, T.A. (2009) "Gendered war and gendered peace: Truth commissions and postconflict gender violence: Lessons from South Africa", *Violence Against Women*, 15: 1169–93.

Bosworth, M., and Fili, A. (2013) "Corrections, gender-specific programming and offender re-entry", in C.M. Renzetti, S.L. Miller, and A.R. Gover (eds.) *Routledge International Handbook of Crime and Gender Studies*, London: Routledge.

Bosworth, M., and Hoyle, C. (eds.) (2011) *What is Criminology?* Oxford: Oxford University Press.

Box, S. (1987) *Recession, Crime, and Punishment*, London: Tavistock.

Brennan, P.K., and Vandenberg, A.L. (2009) "Depictions of female offenders in front-page newspaper stories: The importance of race/ethnicity", *International Journal of Social Inquiry*, 2: 141–75.

Britton, D.M. (1997) "Gendered organizational logic: Policy and practice in men's and women's prisons", *Gender & Society*, 11: 796–818.

—— (2000) "Feminism in criminology: Engendering the outlaw", *Annals of the American Academy of Social Sciences*, 571: 57–76.

—— (2003) *At Work in the Iron Cage: The Prison as Gendered Organization*, New York: New York University Press.

Bronstein, P. (1988) "Father-child interactions", in P. Bronstein and C.P. Cowan (eds.) *Fatherhood Today: Men's Changing Roles in the Family*, New York: John Wiley.

Brookman, F., Mullins, C., Bennett, T., and Wright, R. (2007) "Gender, motivation, and the accomplishment of street robbery in the United Kingdom", *British Journal of Criminology*, 47: 861–84.

Brown, L.M., Chesney-Lind, M., and Stein, N. (2007) "Patriarchy matters: Toward a gendered theory of teen violence and victimization", *Violence Against Women*, 13: 1249–73.

Bufkin, J. (1999) "Bias crime as gendered behavior", *Social Justice*, 26: 155–76.

Burawoy, M. (1996) "The power of feminism", *Perspectives: The ASA Theory Section Newsletter*, 18(3): 4–6.

Bureau of Justice Statistics (2012) *Local Police*. Retrieved from www.bjs.ojp.usdoj.gov/index.cfm?ty=tp&tid=71.

Burgess-Proctor, A. (2006) "Intersections of race, class, gender, and crime: Future directions for feminist criminology", *Feminist Criminology*, 1: 27–47.

Burns, A.L., Mitchell, G., and Obradovich, S. (1989) "Of sex roles and strollers: Female and male attention to toddlers at the zoo", *Sex Roles*, 20: 309–15.

Butler, J. (1990) *Gender Trouble: Feminism and the Subversion of Identity*, New York: Routledge.

Cain, M., and Hunt, A. (1979) *Marx and Engels on Law*, London: Academic Press.

Callahan, J.L. (2009) "Manifestations of power and control: Trainings as the catalyst for scandal at the United States Air Force Academy", *Violence Against Women*, 15: 1149–68.

Campbell, R. (ed.) (2011a) Special issue: "Methodological advances in recruitment and assessment", *Violence Against Women*, 17(3).

—— (ed.) (2011b) Special issue: "Methodological advances in analytic techniques for longitudinal designs and evaluations of community interventions", *Violence Against Women*, 17(4).

Campbell, R., Adams, A., Wasco, S., Ahrens, C., and Sefl, T. (2010) "'What has it been like for you to talk with me today?' The impact of participating in interview research on rape survivors", *Violence Against Women*, 17: 253–61.

Campbell, R., Patterson, D., and Bybee, D. (2011) "Using mixed methods to evaluate a community intervention for sexual assault survivors: A methodological tale", *Violence Against Women*, 17: 376–88.

—— (2012) "Prosecution of adult sexual assault cases: A longitudinal analysis of the impact of a Sexual Assault Nurse Examiner program", *Violence Against Women*, 18: 223–44.

Caringella, S. (2008) *Addressing Rape Reform in Law and Practice*, New York: Columbia University Press.

Carlen, P. (1988) *Women, Crime, and Poverty*, Bristol, PA: Open University Press.

—— (1995) "Women, crime, feminism, and realism", in N. Naffine (ed.) *Gender, Crime and Feminism*, Aldershot, UK: Dartmouth Publishing Company.

—— (2011) "Against evangelism in academic criminology: For criminology as a scientific art", in M. Bosworth and C. Hoyle (eds.) *What is Criminology?*, Oxford: Oxford University Press.

Carlson, B.E., and Worden, A.P. (2002) *Public Opinion about Domestic Violence*, Washington, DC: U.S. Department of Justice.

Catalyst (2012) *Women in Law in the U.S.* Retrieved from www.catalyst.org/publication/246/women-in-law-in-the-us.

CBC News Online (2006, May 30) "Women in the military – International". Retrieved from www.cbc.ca/news/background/military-international/

Cermele, J. (2010) "Telling our stories: The importance of women's narratives of resistance", *Violence Against Women*, 16: 1162–72.

Chesney-Lind, M. (1980) "Rediscovering Lilith: Misogyny and the 'new' female criminal", in C.T. Griffiths and M. Nance (eds.) *The Female Offender*, Burnaby, BC, Canada: Simon Fraser University.

—— (1986) "Women and Crime: The Female Offender", *Signs*, 12: 78–96.

—— (1997) *The Female Offender*, Thousand Oaks, CA: SAGE.

—— (2006) "Patriarchy, crime, and justice: Feminist criminology in an era of backlash", *Feminist Criminology*, 1: 6–26.

Chesney-Lind, M., and Shelden, R.G. (1992) *Girls, Delinquency, and Juvenile Justice*, Pacific Grove, CA: Brooks/Cole.

Children's Defense Fund (2008) *Child Poverty in America*. Retrieved from www.childrensdefensefund.org/child-research-data-publications/data/Child_Poverty_in_America_August_2008_ID8341.pdf.

Cohen, A.K. (1966) *Deviance and Control*, Englewood Cliffs, NJ: Prentice-Hall.

Collins, P.H. (1986) "Learning from the outsider within: The sociological significance of black feminist thought", *Social Problems*, 33: 14–32.

—— (1990) *Black Feminist Thought*, New York: Routledge.

—— (1997) "Comment on Hekman's 'Truth and method: Feminist standpoint theory revisited': Where's the power?" *Signs*, 22: 375–81.

—— (2000) *Black Feminist Thought*, 2nd ed., New York: Routledge.

—— (2012) "Looking back, moving ahead: Scholarship in service to social justice", *Gender & Society*, 26: 14–22.
Collins, S.C. (2006) "Portrait in blue: A demographic and behavioral profile of police sexual harassers", *Women & Criminal Justice*, 18: 79–106.
Commission on Professionals in Science and Technology (1987) *Professional Women and Minorities*, Washington, DC: Commission on Professionals in Science and Technology.
Connell, R.W. (1995) *Masculinities*, Berkeley: University of California Press.
Cott, N.F. (1986) "Feminist theory and feminist movements: The past before us", in J. Mitchell, and A. Oakley (eds.) *What is Feminism? A Reexamination*, New York: Pantheon.
—— (1987) *The Grounding of Modern Feminism*, New Haven, CT: Yale University Press.
Cowan, R.L., and Bochantin, J.E. (2009) "Pregnancy and motherhood on the Thin Blue Line: Female police officers' perspectives on motherhood in a highly masculinized work environment", *Women and Language*, 32: 22–30.
Crabtree, S., and Nsubuga, F. (2012, July 6) "Women feel less safe than men in many developed countries" (Gallup Poll). Retrieved from www.gallup.com/poll/155402/Women-Feel-Less-Safe-Men-Developed-Countries.aspx.
Craven, D. (1996) *Female Victims of Violent Crime*, Washington, DC: U.S. Department of Justice, Bureau of Justice Statistics.
Crenshaw, K. (1994) "Mapping the margins: Intersectionality, identity politics, and violence against women of color", in M.A. Fineman and R. Mykitiuk (eds.) *The Public Nature of Private Violence*, New York: Routledge.
Curran, D.J., and Renzetti, C.M. (1993) *Theories of Crime*, 1st ed., Boston: Allyn and Bacon.
Currie, E. (1992) "Retreatism, minimalism, realism: Three styles of reasoning on crime and drugs in the United States", in J. Lowman and B.D. MacLean (eds.) *Realist Criminology: Crime Control and Policing in the 1990s*, Toronto: University of Toronto Press.
—— (2007) "Against marginality: Arguments for public criminology", *Theoretical Criminology*, 11: 175–90.
Daly, K. (1989) "Gender and varieties of white-collar crime", *Criminology*, 27: 769–94.
—— (1993) "Class-race-gender: Sloganeering in search of meaning", *Social Justice*, 20: 56–71.
—— (1994) *Gender, Crime and Punishment*, New Haven, CT: Yale University Press.

—— (1997) "Different ways of conceptualizing sex/gender in feminist theory and their implications for feminist criminology", *Theoretical Criminology*, 1: 25–51.

Daly, K., and Chesney-Lind, M. (1988) "Feminism and Criminology", *Justice Quarterly*, 5: 497–538.

Daly, K., and Stephens, D. (1995) "The 'dark figure' of criminology: Towards a black and multi-ethnic feminist agenda for theory and research", in N.H. Rafter, and F. Heidensohn (eds.) *International Feminist Perspectives in Criminology: Engendering a Discipline*, Philadephia: Open University Press.

Dasgupta, S.D. (2002) "A framework for understanding women's use of nonlethal violence in intimate heterosexual relationships", *Violence Against Women*, 8: 1364–89.

Davis, N.J. (1993) "Female youth homelessness – systematic gender control", *Socio-Legal Bulletin*, Summer: 22–31.

DeJong, C. (2013) "Policing styles, officer gender and decision making", in C.M. Renzetti, S.L. Miller, and A.R. Gover (eds.) *Routledge International Handbook of Crime and Gender Studies*, London: Routledge.

DeKeseredy, W.S. (ed.) (2000) Special issue: "Current Violence against Women Issues in Canada: Perspectives of Profeminist Men", *Violence Against Women*, 6(9).

—— (2011a) *Violence against Women: Myths, Facts, and Controversies*, Toronto: University of Toronto Press.

—— (2011b) *Contemporary Critical Criminology*, London: Routledge.

DeKeseredy, W.S., and Dragiewicz, M. (2013) "Gaps in knowledge and emerging areas in gender and crime studies", in C.M. Renzetti, S.L. Miller, and A.R. Gover (eds.) *Routledge International Handbook of Crime and Gender Studies*, London: Routledge.

DeKeseredy, W.S., and Schwartz, M.D. (1996) *Contemporary Criminology*, Belmont, CA: Wadsworth.

—— (2010) "Friedman economic policies, social exclusion, and crime: Toward a gendered left realist subcultural theory", *Crime, Law and Social Change*, 54: 159–70.

Division on Women and Crime (2011) "History". Retrieved from http://ascdwc.com/history/

Dodge, M. (2009) *Women and White-Collar Crime*, Upper Saddle River, NJ: Prentice-Hall.

—— (2013) "Where are the women in white collar crime?", in C.M. Renzetti, S.L. Miller, and A.R. Gover (eds.) *Routledge International Handbook of Crime and Gender Studies*, London: Routledge.

Dodge, M., and Geis, G. (2003) *Stealing Dreams: A Fertility Clinic Scandal*, Boston: Northeastern University Press.

Dorworth, V.E., and Henry, M. (1992) "Optical illusions: The visual representation of blacks and women in introductory criminal justice textbooks", *Journal of Criminal Justice Education*, 3: 251–60.

Dragiewicz, M. (2011) *Equality with a Vengeance: Men's Rights Groups, Battered Women, and Antifeminist Backlash*, Boston: Northeastern University Press.

Dutton, D.G. (2006) *Rethinking Domestic Violence*, Vancouver, Canada: University of British Columbia Press.

Dylan, A., Regehr, C., and Alaggia, R. (2008) "And justice for all? Aboriginal victims of sexual assault", *Violence Against Women*, 14: 678–96.

Eager, P.W. (2008) *From Freedom Fighters to Terrorists: Women and Political Violence*, Aldershot, UK: Ashgate.

Edin, K., and Kissane, R.J. (2010) "Poverty and the American family: A decade in review", *Journal of Marriage and Family*, 72: 460–79.

Edin, K., and Lein, L. (1997) *Making Ends Meet*, New York: Russell Sage Foundation.

Ehrenreich, B. (2001) *Nickel and Dimed: On (Not) Getting by in America*, New York: Metropolitan Books/Henry Holt.

Elam, D. (1994) *Feminism and Deconstruction: Ms. En Abyme*, New York: Routledge.

Engels, F. (1845) *The Condition of the Working Class in England*, New York: International Publishers.

Estrich, S. (1988) *Real Rape*, Cambridge, MA: Harvard University Press.

European Commission (2010) *Domestic Violence against Women Report.* Special Eurobarometer 344. Retrieved from www.ec.europa.eu/public_opinion/archives/ebs_344_en.pdf.

Evans, S.M. (1979) *Personal Politics: The Roots of the Women's Liberation Movement in the Civil Rights Movement and the New Left*, New York: Knopf.

Fagan, J., and Freeman, R.B. (1999) "Crime and work", in M. Tonry (ed.) *Crime and Justice: A Review of Research*, Chicago: University of Chicago Press.

Farrell, A.S. (2000) "Police administrators and supervisors", in N.H. Rafter (ed.) *Encyclopedia of Women and Crime*, Phoenix, AZ: Oryx Press.

Fedders, B. (1997) "Lobbying for mandatory-arrest policies: Race, class and the politics of the battered women's movement", *New York University Review of Law and Social Change*, 23: 281–300.

Ferraro, K.J. (2003) "The words change but the melody lingers: The persistence of Battered Woman Syndrome in criminal cases involving battered women", *Violence Against Women*, 9: 110–29.

—— (2006) *Neither Angels nor Demons: Women, Crime and Victimization*, Boston: Northeastern University Press.

Flavin, J., and Artz, L. (2013) "Understanding women, gender, and crime: Some historical and international developments", in C.M. Renzetti, S.L. Miller, and R.A. Gover (eds.) *Routledge International Handbook of Crime and Gender Studies*, London: Routledge.

Flynn, N.T., Hanks, R.S., and Gurley, L. (2007) "Stirred, shaken or blended? Gender differences in processing and treatment of juvenile offenders", *Women and Criminal Justice*, 18: 17–36.

Frankenberg, R. (1993) *White Women, Race Matters: The Social Construction of Whiteness*, Minneapolis: University of Minnesota Press.

Freud, S. (1933) *New Introductory Lectures on Psychoanalysis*, Binghamton, NY: Vail-Ballou Press.

Friedan, B. (1963) *The Feminine Mystique*, New York: W.W. Norton.

Friedrichs, D.O. (2009) "Critical criminology", in J.M. Miller (ed.) *21st Century Criminology: A Reference Handbook, Volume 1*, Thousand Oaks, CA: SAGE.

Frost, N.A., and Clear, T.R. (2007) "Doctoral education in criminology and criminal justice", *Journal of Criminal Justice Education*, 18: 35–42.

Gabbidon, S., Greene, H.T., and Wilder, K. (2004) "Still excluded? An update on the status of African American scholars in the discipline of criminology and criminal justice", *Journal of Research in Crime and Delinquency*, 41: 384–406.

Garfield, G. (2005) *Knowing What We Know: African American Women's Experiences of Violence and Violation*, New Brunswick, NJ: Rutgers University Press.

Garrison, C.G., McClelland, F., Dambrot, F., and Casey, K.A. (1992) "Gender balancing the criminal justice curriculum and classroom", *Journal of Criminal Justice Education*, 3: 203–22.

Gates, M.J. (1976) "Occupational segregation and the law", in M. Blaxall and B. Reagan (eds) *Women and the Workplace*, Chicago: University of Chicago Press.

Gelsthorpe, L., and Morris, A. (1988) "Feminism and criminology in Britain", *British Journal of Criminology*, 28: 93–110.

General Accounting Office (2011) *Military Justice: Oversight and Better Collaboration Needed for Sexual Assault Investigations and Adjudications*, Washington, DC: General Accounting Office.

Gerber, J., and Weeks, S.L. (1992) "Women as victims of corporate crime: A call for research on a neglected topic", *Deviant Behavior*, 13: 325–47.

Gibbons, D. (1994) *Talking about Crime and Criminals: Problems and Issues in Theory Development in Criminology*, Englewood Cliffs, NJ: Prentice Hall.

Gilbert, E. (2000) "Police officers, women of color as", in N.H. Rafter (ed.) *Encyclopedia of Women and Crime*, Phoenix, AZ: Oryx Press.

Gilbert, E., and Tatum, B.L. (1999) "African American women in the criminal justice academy: Characteristics, perceptions, and coping strategies", *Journal of Criminal Justice Education*, 10: 231–46.

Gilfus, M.E. (1993) "From victims to survivors to offenders: Women's routes of entry and immersion into street crime", *Women and Criminal Justice*, 4: 63–89.

Gillum, T.L. (2002) "Exploring the link between stereotypic images and intimate partner violence in the African American community", *Violence Against Women*, 8: 64–86.

Gonzalez-Perez, M. (2008) *Women and Terrorism: Female Activity in Domestic and International Terror Groups*, New York: Routledge.

Goodey, J. (1997) "Boys don't cry: Masculinities, fear of crime, and fearlessness", *British Journal of Criminology*, 37: 401–18.

Goodmark, L. (2012) *A Troubled Marriage: Domestic Violence and the Legal System*, New York: New York University Press.

Goodstein, L. (1992) "Feminist perspectives and the criminal justice curriculum", *Journal of Criminal Justice Education*, 3: 165–81.

Gordon, V.V. (1987) *Black Women, Feminism, and Black Liberation: Which Way?* Chicago: Third World Press.

Gould, S.J. (1981) *The Mismeasure of Man*, New York: W.W. Norton.

Gover, A.R., Paul, D.P., and Dodge, M. (2011) "Law enforcement officers' attitudes about domestic violence", *Violence Against Women*, 17: 619–36.

Gracia, E., Garcia, F., and Lila, M. (2008) "Police involvement in cases of intimate partner violence against women: The influence of perceived severity and personal responsibility", *Violence Against Women*, 14: 697–714.

Grant, J. (1993) *Fundamental Feminism: Contesting the Core Concepts of Feminist Theory*, New York: Routledge.

Griffin, M.L. (2013) "From resistance to integration: The influence of gender in the corrections work environment", in C.M. Renzetti, S.L. Miller, and R.A. Gover (eds.) *Routledge International Handbook of Crime and Gender Studies*, London: Routledge.

Griffin, M.L., Armstrong, G., and Hepburn, J. (2005) "Correctional officers' perceptions of equitable treatment in the masculinized prison environment", *Criminal Justice Review*, 30: 189–206.

Gruber, J.E., and Morgan, P. (eds.) (2005) *In the Company of Men: Male Dominance and Sexual Harassment*, Boston: Northeastern University Press.

Grzywacz, J.G., Rao, P., Gentry, A., Marin, A., and Arcury, T.A. (2009) "Acculturation and conflict in Mexican immigrants' intimate partnerships: The role of women's labor force participation", *Violence Against Women*, 15: 1213–26.

Guerino, P., Harrison, P.M., and Sabol, W.J. (2012) *Prisoners in 2010*, Washington, DC: U.S. Department of Justice, Bureau of Justice Statistics. Retrieved from http://bjs.ojp.usdoj.gov/index.cfm?ty=pbdetail&iid=2230.

Guevara, L., Herz, D., and Spohn, C. (2006) "Gender and juvenile decision making: What role does race play?" *Feminist Criminology*, 1: 258–82.

Hagan, J. (1989) *Structural Criminology*, New Brunswick, NJ: Rutgers University Press.

Hagan, J. (1990) "The structuration of gender and deviance: A power-control theory of vulnerability to crime and the search for deviant role exits", *Canadian Review of Sociology*, 27: 137–56.

Hagan, J., and Kay, F. (1995) *Gender in Practice: A Study of Lawyer's Lives*, New York: Oxford University Press.

Hagan, J., Gillis, A.R., and Simpson, J. (1987) "Class in the household: A power-control theory of gender and delinquency", *American Journal of Sociology*, 90: 1151–78.

Hague, G., and Malos, E. (1993) *Domestic Violence: Action for Change*, Cheltenham: New Clarion Press.

Hall, R.M., and Sandler, B.R. (1985) "A chilly climate in the classroom", in A.G. Sargent (ed.) *Beyond Sex Roles*, New York: West.

Hancock, A. (2011) *Solidarity Politics for Millenials*, New York: Palgrave MacMillan.

Harding, S. (1993) "Rethinking standpoint epistemology: 'What is strong objectivity?'", in L. Alcoff and E. Potter (eds.) *Feminist Epistemologies*, New York: Routledge.

Harris, K. (2012, March) [Commentary on K. G. Muhammad's *The Condemnation of Blackness: Race, Crime, and the Making of Modern Urban America*], Author Meets Critics Session, Annual Meeting of the Academy of Criminal Justice Sciences, New York, NY.

Hautzinger, S.J. (1997) Calling a state a state: Feminist politics and the policing of violence against women in Brazil", *Feminist Issues*, 15(1–2): 3–30.

Heidensohn, F.M. (1968) "The deviance of women: A critique and enquiry", *British Journal of Sociology*, 19: 160–75.

—— (2000) "Police work, history of women in Britain", in N.H. Rafter (ed.) *Encyclopedia of Women and Crime*, Phoenix, AZ: Oryz Press.

Heimer, K., and DeCoster, S. (1999) "The gendering of violent delinquency", *Criminology*, 37: 277–318.

Henry, N. (2010) "The impossibility of bearing witness: Wartime rape and the promise of justice", *Violence Against Women*, 16: 1098–119.

Henry, S. (1999) "Is left realism a useful theory for addressing the problems of crime? No", in J.R. Fuller and E.W. Hickey (eds.) *Controversial Issues in Criminology*, Boston: Allyn and Bacon.
Hess, B.B., and Ferree, M.M. (1987) "Introduction", in B.B. Hess and M.M. Ferree (eds.) *Analyzing Gender*, Newbury Park, CA: SAGE.
Higgenbotham, E. (2012) "Reflections on the early contributions of Patricia Hill Collins", *Gender & Society*, 26: 23–7.
Hill, G., and Crawford, E. (1990) "Women, race and crime", *Criminology*, 28: 601–23.
Hine, D.C., and Thompson, K. (eds.) (1997) *A Shining Thread of Hope: The History of Black Women in America*, New York: Broadway Books.
Holcomb, J.E., Williams, M.R., and Demuth, S. (2004) "White female victims and death penalty disparity research", *Justice Quarterly*, 21: 877–902.
Hollander, J. (2009) "The roots of resistance to women's self-defense", *Violence Against Women*, 15: 574–94.
Horne, P. (2006) "Policewomen: Their first century and new era", *Police Chief*, 73:1–10.
Howard, J.A., and Allen, C. (eds.) (2000) Special issue: "Feminisms at the millennium", *Signs*, 25(4).
Howe, A. (2000) "Postmodern criminology and its feminist discontents", *Australian and New Zealand Journal of Criminology*, 33: 221–36.
Hudson, B. (1998) "Restorative justice: The challenge of sexual and racial violence", *Journal of Law and Society*, 25: 237–56.
Humphries, D. (1999) *Crack Mothers: Pregnancy, Drugs and the Media*, Columbus: Ohio State University Press.
—— (2013) "Media, crime and gender", in C.M. Renzetti, S.L. Miller, and A.R. Gover (eds.) *Routledge International Handbook of Crime and Gender Studies*, London: Routledge.
Inter-Parliamentary Union (2008a) *Women Speakers of National Parliaments: History and the Present.* Retrieved from: www.ipu.org/wmn-e/speakers/htm.
—— (2008b) *Women in National Parliaments: World and Regional Averages.* Retrieved from: www.ipu.org/wmn-e/world.htm.
Jaffe, P.G., Berman, H., and MacQuarrie, B. (2011) "A Canadian model for building university and community partnerships: Centre for Research and Education on Violence Against Women and Children", *Violence Against Women*, 17: 1159–76.
Jones, N. (2009) "'I was aggressive for the streets, pretty for the pictures': Gender, difference, and the inner-city girl", *Gender & Society*, 23: 89–93.
—— (2010) *Between Good and Ghetto: African American Girls and Inner-city Violence*, New Brunswick, NJ: Rutgers University Press.

Jordan, C.E. (ed.) (2011) Special issue: "Building Academic Research Centers to Advance Research on Violence against Women: An Empirical Foundation", *Violence Against Women*, 17(9).

Jordan, J. (2005) "What would MacGyver do? The meaning(s) of resistance and survival", *Violence Against Women*, 11: 531–59.

Jurik, N.C. (1999) "Socialist feminist criminology and social justice", in B.A. Arrigo (ed.) *Social Justice, Criminal Justice*, Belmont, CA: Wadsworth.

Jurik, N.C., and Martin, S.E. (2001) "Femininities, masculinities, and organizational conflict: Women in criminal justice occupations", in C.M. Renzetti and L. Goodstein (eds) *Women, Crime, and Criminal Justice*, Los Angeles: Roxbury.

Jurik, N.C., and Siemsen, C. (2009) " 'Doing gender' as canon or agenda: A symposium on West and Zimmerman", *Gender & Society*, 23: 72–5.

Kaukinen, C. (2004) "Status incompatibility, physical violence, and emotional abuse in intimate relationships", *Journal of Marriage and Family*, 66: 452–71.

Kaukinen, C., and DeMaris, A. (2009) "Sexual assault and current mental health: The role of help-seeking and police response", *Violence Against Women*, 15: 1331–57.

Kazemian, L. (2012) "Pushing back the frontiers of knowledge on desistance from crime", in R. Loeber and B.C. Welsh (eds.) *The Future of Criminology*, Oxford: Oxford University Press.

Keith, B., Layne, J.S., Babchuk, N., and Johnson, K. (2002) "The context of scientific achievement: Sex status, organizational environments, and the timing of publication on scholarship outcomes", *Social Forces*, 80: 1253–82.

Kellerman, B., and Rhode, D.L. (eds.) (2007) *Women and Leadership*, San Francisco: Jossey-Bass.

Kelly, L. (2010) "The (in)credible words of women: False allegations in European rape research", *Violence Against Women*, 16: 1345–55.

Kenney, S.J. (2008) "Thinking about gender and judging", *International Journal of the Legal Profession*, 15: 87–110.

Kessler, S.J. (1996) "The medical construction of gender: Case management of intersexed infants", in B. Laslett, S.G. Kohlstedt, H. Longino, and E. Hammonds (eds.) *Gender and Scientific Authority*, Chicago: University of Chicago Press.

King, D.K. (1988) "Multiple jeopardy, multiple consciousness: The context of black feminist ideology", *Signs*, 14: 42–72.

Klein, D. (1973) "The etiology of female crime: A review of the literature", *Issues in Criminology*, 8: 3–30.

Klein, D., and Kress, J. (1976) "Any woman's blues: A critical overview of women, crime, and the criminal justice system", *Crime and Social Justice*, 5: 34–49.

Krisberg, B. (1975) *Crime and Privilege*, Englewood Cliffs, NJ: Prentice-Hall.

Kruttschnitt, C. (2001) "Gender and violence", in C.M. Renzetti and L. Goodstein (eds.) *Gender, Crime, and Criminal Justice*, Los Angeles: Roxbury.

Kuehnast, K., Oudraat, C.dJ., and Hernes, H. (eds.) (2011) *Women and War: Power and Protection in the 21st Century*, Washington, DC: United States Institute of Peace Press.

Landrine, H. (1985) "Race x class stereotypes of women", *Sex Roles*, 13: 65–75.

Larance, L., and Dasgupta, S.D. (eds) (2012) Special issue: "Heterosexual Battered Women's Use of Non-fatal Force", *Violence Against Women*, 18(9).

Laslett, B., and Brenner, J. (2000) "Twenty-first century academic feminism in the United States: Utopian visions and practical actions", *Signs*, 25: 1231–36.

Lea, J., and Young, J. (1984) *What is to Be Done About Law and Order?* New York: Penguin.

Le Gates, M. (2001) *In Their Time: A History of Feminism in Western Society*, New York: Taylor and Francis.

Lee, H.K. (2009, August 14) "Police face 7 sex discrimination lawsuits", *San Francisco Chronicle*, p. D4.

Lee, S.M. (1993) "Racial classifications and the U.S. census, 1890–1990", *Ethnic and Racial Studies*, 16: 75–94.

Lee-Koo, K. (2011) "Gender-based violence against women in post-invasion Iraq: (Re)Politicizing George W. Bush's silent legacy", *Violence Against Women*, 17: 1619–34.

Leonard, E. (1982) *Women, Crime and Society: A Critique of Criminology Theory*, New York: Longman.

—— (1995) "Theoretical criminology and gender", in B.R. Price and N.J. Sokoloff (eds.) *The Criminal Justice System and Women*, New York: McGraw-Hill.

Lerner, G. (1993) *The Creation of Feminist Consciousness*, New York: Oxford University Press.

Loeber, R., and Welsh, B.C. (eds.) (2012) *The Future of Criminology*, Oxford: Oxford University Press.

Lombroso, C., and Ferrero, W. (1893) *The Female Offender*, New York: Appleton.

Lonsway, K.A., and Archambault, J. (2012) "The 'justice gap' for sexual assault cases: Future directions for research and reform", *Violence Against Women*, 18: 145–68.

Lorber, J. (2005) *Breaking the Bowls: Degendering and Feminist Change*, New York: W.W. Norton.

—— (2009) *Gender Inequality: Feminist Theory and Politics*, New York: Oxford University Press.

Lovenduski, J. (1986) *Women and European Politics*, Amherst: University of Massachusetts Press.

Lynch, M.J., and Groves, W.B. (1986) *A Primer in Radical Criminology*. New York: Harrow & Heston.

McCarthy, B., Hagan, J., and Woodward, T.S. (1999) "In the company of women: Structure and agency in a revised power-control theory of gender and delinquency", *Criminology*, 37: 761–88.

MacDonald, K., and Parke, R.D. (1986) "Parent-child physical play: The effects of sex and age on children and parents", *Sex Roles*, 15: 367–78.

McElrath, K. (1990) "Standing in the shadows: Academic mentoring in criminology", *Journal of Criminal Justice Education*, 1: 135–51.

McIntosh, P. (1983) "Interactive phases of curricular revision: A feminist perspective", *Wellesley Working Papers Series*, no. 124, Wellesley, MA: Wellesley College Center for Research on Women.

MacKinnon, C.A. (1989) *Toward a Feminist Theory of the State*, Cambridge, MA: Harvard University Press.

MacMillan, R., and Gartner, R. (1999) "When she brings home the bacon: Labor force participation and risk of spousal violence against women", *Journal of Marriage and Family*, 61: 947–58.

Mahan, S., and Anthony, A.M. (1992) "Including women in corrections texts", *Journal of Criminal Justice Education*, 3: 261–75.

Maidment, M.R. (2006) "Transgressing boundaries: Feminist perspectives in criminology", in W.S. DeKeseredy and B. Perry (eds.) *Advancing Critical Criminology: Theory and Application*, Lanham, MD: Lexington Books.

Marx, K., and Engels, F. (1948) *The Communist Manifesto*, New York: International Publishers.

Meloy, M.L. (2000) "Police organizations, municipal and state", in N.H. Rafter (ed.) *Encyclopedia of Women and Crime*, Phoenix, AZ: Oryz Press.

Meloy, M.L., Maier, S.L., and Miller, S.L. (2006) "Women on the bench", in C.M. Renzetti, L Goodstein, and S.L. Miller (eds.) *Rethinking Gender, Crime, and Justice*, Los Angeles: Roxbury.

Messerschmidt, J. (1986) *Capitalism, Patriarchy, and Crime*, Totowa, NJ: Rowman & Littlefield.

—— (1993) *Masculinities and Crime*, Lanham, MD: Rowman & Littlefield.

—— (1995) *From Patriarchy to Gender: Feminist Theory, Criminology, and the Challenge of Diversity*, Philadelphia: Open University Press.

—— (1997) *Crime as Structured Social Action: Gender, Race, Class, and Crime in the Making*, Thousand Oaks, CA: SAGE.

—— (2000) *Nine Lives: Adolescent Masculinity, The Body, and Violence*, Boulder, CO: Westview.
—— (2002) "On gang girls, gender, and a structured action theory: A reply to Miller", *Theoretical Criminology*, 6: 461–75.
Miller, E.M. (1986) *Street Woman*, Philadelphia: Temple University Press.
Miller, J. (1998) "Up it up: Gender and the accomplishment of street robbery", *Criminology*, 36: 37–66.
—— (2001) *One of the Guys: Girls, Gangs and Gender*, New York: Oxford University Press.
—— (2002) "The strengths and limits of 'doing gender' for understanding street crime", *Theoretical Criminology*, 6: 433–60.
—— (2008) *Getting Played: African American Girls, Urban Inequality, and Gendered Violence*, New York: New York University Press.
Miller, J.A. (2011) "Social justice work: Purpose-driven social science", *Social Problems*, 58: 1–20.
Miller, S.L. (2005) *Victims as Offenders: The Paradox of Women's Violence in Relationships*, New Brunswick, NJ: Rutgers University Press.
—— (2011) *After the Crime: The Power of Restorative Justice Dialogues between Victims and Violent Offenders*, New York: New York University Press.
Mills, C.W. (1959) *The Sociological Imagination*, New York: Oxford University Press.
Morash, M. (2010) *Women on Probation and Parole: A Feminist Critique of Community Programs and Services*, Boston: Northeastern University Press.
Morash, M., and Chesney-Lind, M. (1991) "A re-formulation and partial test of power-control theory", *Justice Quarterly*, 8: 347–77.
Morash, M., Haarr, R.N., and Gonyea, D.P. (2006) "Workplace problems in police departments and methods of coping: Women at the intersection", in C.M. Renzetti, L. Goodstein, and S.L. Miller (eds.) *Rethinking Gender, Crime, and Justice*, Los Angeles: Roxbury.
Morton, J.B. (1991) "Women correctional officers: A ten year update", in J.B. Morton (ed.) *Change, Challenge, and Choices: Women's Role in Modern Corrections*, Laham, MD: American Correctional Association.
Muhammad, K.G. (2010) *The Condemnation of Blackness: Race, Crime, and the Making of Modern Urban America*, Cambridge, MA: Harvard University Press.
Myers, S.L. (2009, December 28) "Another peril in war zones: Sexual abuse by fellow G.I.'s", *New York Times*, pp. A1, A10.
Naffine, N. (1995) "Criminal conversation", *Law and Critique*, 6: 193–207.

—— (1996) *Feminism and Criminology*, Philadelphia: Temple University Press.

—— (2002) "In praise of legal feminism", *Legal Studies*, 22: 77–101.

Naples, N.A. (2003) *Feminism and Method*, New York: Routledge.

Nash, S.T. (2005). "Through black eyes: African American women's constructions of their experiences with intimate male partner violence", *Violence Against Women*, 11: 1420–40.

"Nature of clothing isn't evidence in rape cases, Florida law says" (1990, June 3) *New York Times*, p. 30.

Nelson, S. (1996) "Constructing and negotiating gender in women's police stations in Brazil", *Latin American Perspectives*, 88: 131–48.

"New Zealand judge: Rape as exciting" (1996, July 7) Wellington, New Zealand: Reuters.

Offen, K. (1988) "Defining feminism: A comparative historical approach", *Signs*, 14: 119–57.

O'Neill, W.L. (1969) *Everyone Was Brave*, New York: Quadrangle.

Patten, R., and Way, L.B. (2011) "White men only? A nationwide examination of diversity courses in the criminal justice discipline", *Race, Gender & Class*, 18: 345–59.

Pearce, F. (1976) *Crimes of the Powerful*, London: Pluto Press.

Perry, B. (2001) *In the Name of Hate: Understanding Hate Crime*, New York: Routledge.

Plant, E.A., Hyde, J.S., Keltner, D., and Devine, P.G. (2000) "The gender stereotyping of emotions", *Psychology of Women Quarterly*, 24: 81–92.

Pleck, E. (1987) *Domestic Tyranny: The Making of American Social Policy against Family Violence from Colonial Times to the Present*, New York: Oxford University Press.

Pollak, O. (1950) *The Criminality of Women*, Philadelphia: University of Pennsylvania Press.

Potter, H. (2006) "An argument for black feminist criminology: Understanding African American women's experiences with intimate partner violence using an integrated approach", *Feminist Criminology*, 1: 106–24.

—— (2008) *Battle Cries: Black Women and Intimate Partner Violence*, New York: New York University Press.

Potter, H., Higgins, G.E., and Gabbidon, S.L. (2011) "The influence of gender, race/ethnicity, and faculty perceptions on scholarly productivity in criminology/criminal justice", *Journal of Criminal Justice Education*, 22: 84–101.

Potter, S.J., and Banyard, V.L. (eds.) (2011) Special issue: "Engaging Communities to End Sexual Violence: Current Research on Bystander-focused Prevention", *Violence Against Women*, 17(6).

Preves, S.E. (2003) *Intersex and Identity: The Contested Self*, New Brunswick, NJ: Rutgers University Press.

Ptacek, J. (2010a) "Resisting co-optation: Three feminist challenges to antiviolence work", in J. Ptacek (ed.) *Restorative Justice and Violence Against Women*, New York: Oxford University Press.

—— (ed.) (2010b) *Restorative Justice and Violence Against Women*, New York: Oxford University Press.

Quester, G.H. (1982) "The problem", in N.L. Goldman (ed.), *Female Soldiers: Combatants or Noncombatants?* Westport, CT: Greenwood Press.

Quinney, R. (1973) *Critique of the Legal Order*, Boston: Little, Brown.

Rabe-Hemp, C.E. (2009) "POLICEwomen or policeWOMEN? Doing gender and police work", *Feminist Criminology*, 4: 114–29.

Radford, J. (1987) "Policing male violence, policing women", in J. Hamner and M. Maynard (eds.) *Violence and Social Control*, Atlantic Highlands, NJ: Humanities Press International.

Radford, J., and Russell, D.E.H. (1992) *Femicide: The Politics of Woman Killing*, New York: Macmillan.

Rafter, N.H. (2000) "Preface", in N.H.Rafter (ed.) *Encyclopedia of Women and Crime*, Phoenix, AZ: Oryz Press.

Raj, A., Silverman, J.G., Wingood, G.M., and DiClemente, R.J. (1999) "Prevalence and correlates of relationship abuse among a community-based sample of low-income African American women", *Violence Against Women*, 5: 272–91.

Rampell, C. (2010) "Women now a majority in U.S. workplace", *New York Times*. Retrieved from www.nytimes.com/2010/02/06/business/economy/06women.html.

Randall, M. (2004) "Domestic violence and the construction of 'ideal victims': Assaulted women's 'image problems' in law", *St. Louis University Public Law Review*, 23: 107–54.

Ransby, B. (2000) "Black feminism at twenty-one: Reflections on the evolution of a national community", *Signs*, 25: 1215–21.

Rasche, C. (1974) "The female offender as an object of criminological research", *Criminal Justice and Behavior*, 1: 301–20.

Reid, G.M. (1994) "Maternal sex-stereotyping of newborns", *Psychological Reports*, 75: 1443–50.

Reiman, J. (1979) *The Rich Get Richer and the Poor Get Prison*, Boston: Allyn and Bacon.

Reinharz, S. (1992) *Feminist Methods in Social Research*, New York: Oxford University Press.

Renzetti, C.M. (1997) "Confessions of a reformed positivist: Feminist participatory research as good social science", in M.D. Schwartz (ed.) *Researching Sexual Violence against Women*, Thousand Oaks, CA: SAGE.

—— (2011a) "Economic issues and intimate partner violence", in C.M. Renzetti, J.L. Edleson, and R.K. Bergen (eds.) *Sourcebook on Violence Against Women*, Thousand Oaks, CA: SAGE.

—— (2011b) "*Women and War*: A commentary". Paper presented at the Annual Meeting of the American Society of Criminology, Washington, DC.

Renzetti, C.M., and Curran, D.J. (1989) *Women, Men, and Society: The Sociology of Gender*, 1st ed., Boston, MA: Allyn and Bacon.

Renzetti, C.M., and Lee, R.M. (eds.) (1993) *Researching Sensitive Topics*, Newbury Park, CA: SAGE.

Renzetti, C.M., Edleson, J.L., and Bergen, R.K. (eds.) (2011) *Sourcebook on Violence Against Women*, 2nd ed., Thousand Oaks, CA: SAGE.

Renzetti, C.M., Curran, D.J., and Meier, S.L. (2012) *Women, Men, and Society: The Sociology of Gender*, 6th ed., Boston: Allyn and Bacon.

Rice, M. (1990) "Challenging orthodoxies in feminist theory: A black feminist critique", in L. Gelsthorpe and A. Morris (eds.) *Feminist Perspectives in Criminology*, Philadelphia: Open University Press.

Rice, S.K., Terry, K.J., Miller, H.V., and Ackerman, A.R. (2007) "Research trajectories of female scholars in criminology and criminal justice", *Journal of Criminal Justice Education*, 18: 360–84.

Richie, B. (1996) *Compelled to Crime*, New York: Routledge.

—— (2005) "A black feminist reflection on the antiviolence movement", in N.J. Sokoloff, and C. Pratt (eds.) *Domestic Violence at the Margins: Readings on Race, Class, Gender, and Culture*, New Brunswick, NJ: Rutgers University Press.

—— (2012) *Arrested Justice: Black Women, Violence, and America's Prison Nation,* New York: New York University Press.

Risman, B.J. (2004) "Gender as social structure", *Gender & Society*, 18: 429–50.

—— (2009) "From doing to undoing: Gender as we know it", *Gender & Society*, 23: 81–4.

Rivara, F.P. (2012) "The future of preventive public health: Implications of brain violence research", in R. Loeber and B.C. Welsh (eds.) *The Future of Criminology*, Oxford: Oxford University Press.

Robina Institute of Criminal Law and Criminal Justice (2012) "Crime and justice in America, 1975–2025", Conference brochure, Minneapolis: University of Minnesota Law School.

Rojek, J., and Decker, S.H. (2009) "Examining racial disparity in the police discipline process", *Police Quarterly*, 4: 388–407.

Rosen, R. (2000) *The World Split Open: How the Modern Women's Movement Changed America*, New York: Viking.

Rudy, K. (2000) "Difference and indifference: A U.S. feminist response to global politics", *Signs*, 25: 1051–54.

Rupp, L.J., and Taylor, V. (1999) "Forging a feminist identity in an international movement: A collective identity approach to twentieth-century feminism", *Signs*, 24: 363–86.

Rynbrandt, L.J., and Kramer, R.C. (1995) "Hybrid nonwomen and corporate violence: The silicone breast implant case", *Violence Against Women*, 1: 206–27.

Sadler, A.G., Booth, B.M., Nielson, D., and Doebbling, B.N. (2000) "Health-related consequences of physical and sexual violence: Women in the military", *Obstetrics and Gynecology*, 96: 473–80.

Samborn, H.V. (2002) *Gender Bias in the Courts: Working Toward Change*. Chicago: American Bar Association.

Sandler, B.R., and Hall, R.M. (1986) *The Campus Climate Revisited: Chilly for Women Faculty, Administrators, and Graduate Students*, Washington, DC: Project on the Status and Education of Women.

Scarborough, K.E. (2000) "Police work and civil rights", in N.H. Rafter (ed.) *Encyclopedia of Women and Crime*, Phoenix, AZ: Oryz Press.

Schechter, S. (1982) *Women and Male Violence: The Visions and Struggles of the Battered Women's Movement*, Boston: South End Press.

Scherer, M. (2010) "The new sheriffs of Wall Street", *Time Magazine*. Retrieved from www.time.com/time/magazine/article/0,9171, 1989144,00.html.

Schulz, D.M. (2000) "Police work, history of women in, USA", in N.H. Rafter (ed.) *Encyclopedia of Women and Crime*, Phoenix, AZ: Oryx Press.

Schur, E.M. (1984) *Labeling Women Deviant: Gender, Stigma, and Social Control*, New York: Random House.

Schwendinger, J., and Schwendinger, H. (1983). *Rape and Inequality*. Newbury Park, CA: SAGE.

Scott, H. (1974) *Does Socialism Liberate Women?* Boston: Beacon Press.

Shepard, M.F., and Pence, E.L. (1999) "An introduction: Developing a coordinated community response", in M.F. Shepard and E.L. Pence (eds.) *Coordinating Community Responses to Domestic Violence: Lessons from Duluth and Beyond*, Thousand Oaks, CA: SAGE.

Shouse Law Group (2012) "California three strikes law explained by criminal defense attorneys". Retrieved from http://www.shouselaw.com/three-strikes.html.

Siegel, J.A., and Williams, L.M. (2003) "The relationship between child sexual abuse and female delinquency and crime: A prospective study", *Journal of Research in Crime and Delinquency*, 40: 71–94.

Siemsen, C. (2006) "Women criminal lawyers", in C.M. Renzetti, L. Goodstein, and S.L. Miller (eds.) *Rethinking Gender, Crime, and Justice*, Los Angeles: Roxbury.

Siemsen, C., and Candela, K. (2013) "Gender and minority representation at the bar and on the bench", in C.M. Renzetti, S.L. Miller, and A.R.

Gover (eds.) *Routledge International Handbook of Crime and Gender Studies*, London: Routledge.

Simon, R.J. (1975) *Women and Crime*, Washington, DC: U.S. Government Printing Office.

Simpson, S.S. (1989) "Feminist theory, crime, and justice", *Criminology*, 27: 605–631.

—— (1991) "Caste, class and violent crime: Explaining differences in female offending", *Criminology*, 33: 47–81.

Smart, C. (1976) *Women, Crime, and Criminology*, London: Routledge Kegan Paul.

—— (1982) "Review", *Critical Social Policy*, 2: 99–101.

—— (1990) "Feminist approaches to criminology: Or postmodern woman meets atavistic man", in L. Gelsthorpe and A. Morris (eds.) *Feminist Perspectives in Criminology*, Milton Keynes, UK: Open University Press.

Smith, B.A. (2000) "Female crime, patterns and trends in, USA", in N.H. Rafter (ed.) *Encyclopedia of Women and Crime*, Phoenix, AZ: Oryz Press.

Smith, D.E. (1996) "Response to Judith Stacey's and Barrie Thorne's essay", *Perspectives: The ASA Theory Section Newsletter*, 18(3): 3–4.

Snell, C., Sorenson, J., Rodriguez, J.J., and Kuanliang, A. (2009) "Gender differences in research productivity among criminal justice and criminology scholars", *Journal of Criminal Justice*, 37: 288–95.

Soares, R., *et al.* (2010) *2010 Catalyst Census: Fortune 500 Women Executive Officers and Top Earners*. Retrieved from: www.catalyst.org/fle/412/2010_us_census_women_executive_of-ficers_and_top_earners_final.pdf.

Sommers, C.H. (1995) *Who Stole Feminism?* New York: Simon and Schuster.

—— (2012, January 27) "How the CDC is overstating sexual violence in the U.S.", *Washington Post*, Retrieved from: www.washingtonpost.com/opinions/cdc-study-on-sexual-violence-in-the-us-overstates-the-problem/2012/01/25/gIQAHRKPWQ_story.html.

Spohn, C., and Brennan, P.K. (2013) "Sentencing and punishment", in C.M. Renzetti, S.L. Miller, and A.R. Gover (eds.) *Routledge International Handbook of Crime and Gender Studies*, London: Routledge.

Spohn, C., and Tellis, K. (2012) The criminal justice system's response to sexual violence", *Violence Against Women*, 169–92.

St. Germain, T., and Dewey, S. (eds.) (2012) *Conflict-Related Sexual Violence: International Law, Local Responses*, Stirling, VA: Kumarian Press.

Stacey, J. (1986) "Are feminists afraid to leave home? The challenge of conservative pro-family feminism", in J. Mitchell and A. Oakley (eds.) *What is Feminism? A Reexamination*, New York: Pantheon.

—— (2000) "Is academic feminism an oxymoron?" *Signs*, 25: 1189–94.
Stacey, J., and Thorne, B. (1996) "Is sociology still missing its feminist revolution?" *Perspectives: The ASA Section Newsletter*, 18(3): 1–3.
Stack, S. (2002) "Gender and scholarly productivity: The case of criminal justice", *Journal of Criminal Justice*, 30: 175–82.
Stanko, E.A. (1986) *Intimate Intrusions*, London: Routledge and Kegan Paul.
—— (1992) "Intimidating education: Sexual harassment in criminology", *Journal of Criminal Justice Education*, 3: 331–40.
—— (1996) "Warnings to women: Police advice and women's safety in Britain", *Violence Against Women*, 2: 5–24.
—— (2001) "Women, danger, and criminology", in C.M. Renzetti and L. Goodstein (eds.) *Women, Crime, and Criminal Justice*, Los Angeles: Roxbury.
Stark, E. (2007) *Coercive Control: How Men Entrap Women in Personal Life*, New York: Oxford University Press.
Steffensmeier, D.J. (1978) "Crime and the contemporary woman: An analysis of changing levels of female property crime", *Social Forces*, 57: 566–84.
—— (1982)"Trends in female crime: It's still a man's world", in B.R. Price and N.J. Sokoloff (eds.) *The Criminal Justice System and Women*, New York: Clark Boardman.
Steffensmeier, D.J., and Cobb, M.J. (1981) "Sex differences in urban arrest patterns, 1934–1979", *Social Problems*, 29: 37–50.
Stephan, J.J. (2008) *Census of State and Federal Correctional Facilities, 2005*. Washington, DC: Bureau of Justice Statistics.
Stohr, M.K. (2006) "'Yes, I've paid the price, but look how much I gained': The struggle and status of women correctional officers", in C.M. Renzetti, L. Goodstein, and S.L. Miller (eds.) *Rethinking Gender, Crime, and Justice*, Los Angeles: Roxbury.
Straus, M.A. (2007) "Processes explaining the concealment and distortion of evidence on gender symmetry in partner violence", *European Journal on Criminal Policy and Research*, 13: 227–32.
Stroud, A. (2012) "Good guys with guns: Hegemonic masculinity and concealed handguns", *Gender & Society*, 26: 216–38.
"Suffragette's racial remark haunts college" (1996, 5 May), *New York Times*, p. 30.
Taylor, I., Walton, P., and Young, J. (1973) *The New Criminology*, New York: Harper Colophone Books.
Taylor, V. (1990) "The continuity of the American women's movement: An elite-sustained stage", in G. West and R.L. Blumberg (eds.) *Women and Social Protest*, New York: Oxford University Press.

Thomas, G.D., and Hollenshead, C. (2001) "Resisting from the margins: The coping strategies of black women and other women faculty of color at a research university", *Journal of Negro Education*, 70: 166–75.

Thomas, W.I. (1923) *The Unadjusted Girl*, New York: Harper and Row.

Thompson, B. (2002) "Multiracial feminism: Recasting the chronology of second wave feminism", *Feminist Studies*, 28: 337–60.

Thompson, R.A. (2006) "Black skin, brass shields: Assessing the presumed marginalization of black law enforcement executives", *American Journal of Criminal Justice*, 30: 163–75.

Thorne, B. (2000) "A telling time for Women's Studies", *Signs*, 25: 1183–8.

Tolman, R.M., and Edleson, J.L. (2011) "Intervening with men for violence prevention", in C.M. Renzetti, J.L. Edleson, and R.K. Bergen (eds.) *Sourcebook on Violence against Women*, Thousand Oaks, CA: SAGE.

True, J. (2012) *The Political Economy of Violence against Women*, New York: Oxford University Press.

Truman, J.L. (2011) *Criminal Victimization, 2010*, Washington, DC: U.S. Department of Justice, Bureau of Justice Statistics.

Turner, C.S.V. (2002) "Women of color in academe: Living with multiple marginality", *Journal of Higher Education*, 73: 74–93.

U.S. Department of Education (1986) *Digest of Education Statistics*, Washington, DC: Government Printing Office.

—— (2012) "Degrees awarded in homeland security, law enforcement, and firefighting, U.S. colleges and universities, sex and race and ethnicity, 2009–10". Retrieved from www.nces.ed.gov/programs/digest/d11/tables/

—— (2012) "Law degrees conferred by U.S. degree granting institutions, sex and race, 2009–10". Retrieved from www.nces.ed.gov/programs/digest/d11/tables/

U.S. Department of Justice and U.S. Department of Health and Human Services (1996) *The Validity and Use of Evidence Concerning Battering and Its Effects in Criminal Trials*, Washington, DC: US. Department of Justice.

Walby, S. (1990) *Theorizing Patriarchy*, Cambridge: Basil Blackwell.

Walsh, A. (2011) *Feminist Criminology through a Biosocial Lens*, Durham, NC: Carolina Academic Press.

Websdale, N. (2001) *Policing the Poor: From Slave Plantation to Public Housing*, Boston: Northeastern University Press.

Wesely, J. K., and Wright, J. D. (2009) "From the inside out: Efforts by homeless women to disrupt cycles of crime and violence", *Women and Criminal Justice*, 19: 217–34.

West, C., and Fenstermaker, S. (1995) "Doing difference", *Gender & Society*, 9: 8–37.
West, C., and Zimmerman, D.H. (1987) "Doing gender", *Gender & Society*, 1: 125–51.
—— (2009) "Accounting for doing gender", *Gender & Society*, 23: 112–22.
Widom, C.S., and Maxfield, M.C. (2001) *An Update on the "Cycle of Violence"*, Washington, DC: U.S. Department of Justice.
Williams, M.R., Demuth, S., and Holcomb, J.E. (2007) "Understanding the influence of victim gender in death penalty cases: The importance of victim race, sex-related victimization, and jury decision making", *Criminology*, 45: 865–91.
Wing, A.K. (ed.) (2003) *Critical Race Feminism: A Reader* (2nd ed.), New York: New York University Press.
Wonders, N.A. (1999) "Postmodern feminist criminology and social justice", in B.A. Arrigo (ed.) *Social Justice, Criminal Justice*, Belmont, CA: Wadsworth.
Wood, K. (2012, April/May) "Women of color, the pressure not to report, and sisterhood", *Domestic Violence Report*, 17: 49–50, 57–9.
Wright, R.A. (1992) "From vamps to tramps to teases to flirts: Stereotypes of women in criminology textbooks, 1956 to 1965 and 1981 to 1990", *Journal of Criminal Justice Education*, 3: 223–36.
Young, J. (1988) "Radical criminology in Britain: The emergence of a competing paradigm", *British Journal of Criminology*, 28: 159–83.
Yuval-Davis, N. (2012) "Dialogical epistemology – an intersectional resistance to the 'oppression olympics'", *Gender & Society*, 26: 46–54.
Zupan, L.L. (1992) "Men guarding women: An analysis of the employment of male correction officers in prisons for women", *Journal of Criminal Justice*, 20: 297–309.

Index